Terence

Twayne's World Authors Series
Latin Literature

Philip Levine, Editor

University of California, Los Angeles

TWAS 745

MS C: folio 29 verso (*Eun.* 765 sqq.)
(vat. lat. 3868). *Photograph courtesy of La Biblioteca Apostolica Vaticana.*

Terence

By Walter E. Forehand

Florida State University

Twayne Publishers • *Boston*

Terence

Walter E. Forehand

Copyright © 1985 by G. K. Hall & Company
All Rights Reserved
Published by Twayne Publishers
A Division of G. K. Hall & Company
70 Lincoln Street
Boston, Massachusetts 02111

Book Production by Elizabeth Todesco
Book Design by Barbara Anderson

Printed on permanent/durable acid-free
paper and bound in the United States of
America.

Library of Congress Cataloging in Publication Data

Forehand, Walter.
    Terence.   *209919*

    (Twayne's world authors series; TWAS 745. Latin
literature)
    Bibliography: p. 141
    Includes index.
    1. Terence—Criticism and interpretation.   I. Title.
II. Series: Twayne's world authors series; TWAS 745.
III. Series: Twayne's world authors series. Latin literature.
PA6768.F6   1985   872'.01   85-743
ISBN 0-8057-6593-X

Mark et John, filiis optime merentibus

Contents

About the Author

Walter Eugene Forehand is professor of Classics and chairman of the Department of Classics at the Florida State University, Tallahassee. He has been teaching there since 1966 and has covered a wide range of subjects in classical literature and culture during his years in the classroom. His published papers deal with classical literature, comparative literary studies, and pedogogy. His special interest, however, has been classical drama and its influence. He has worked on Euripides and Molière and, of course, his principal authors, Plautus and Terence.

Preface

An enthusiast might state boldly that Terence has been Western drama's most influential playwright. In fact, placed in proper perspective, such an assertion is not particularly bold. Given that the influence of the Greek stage came to Europe late (except indirectly through Plautus, Terence, and Seneca) and that comedy has populated the Western stage rather more densely than the tragic or serious play, and considering the very great influence of classical culture in all areas of Western thinking, we can conclude that Terence's only serious rival in "volume" of influence is Plautus.

We must remind ourselves that tastes have changed often through the centuries. The modern era tends to consider "serious" plays more significant than comedies; and in comedy it gives greater attention to pieces that, like Aristophanes' plays, deal with clear-cut political, social, or philosophical issues. In other periods, for example the eighteenth century in England, sophisticated comedy of manners dealing with bourgeois subjects has been more in vogue. A playwright such as Aristophanes may be considered a bit too crude, both morally and dramatically. For such periods Terence has provided a much-valued model for plot material and dramatic theory.

This study strives to present a balanced approach to the plays of Terence, considering the main lines of critical opinion always, but willingly offering new observations, especially on matters of literary interpretation. There has not been a volume in English devoted solely to the study of Terence for sixty years; clearly, the present effort cannot summarize all the work that has been done in the meantime, but it may be able to fill the need for a general, up-to-date survey of one of Western drama's important poets. The reader who does not specialize in classical studies may be relieved to come to Terence without having to confront a body of periodical literature and Continental scholarship; the more specialized reader may wish an overview before dealing directly with the scholarship on which the present volume has drawn.

An outline structure has been used throughout. There has been an effort to make units self-contained; for example, each play is treated in a separate essay, divided into sections on plot, structure, character, and theme, which are in turn subdivided according to the needs of that piece. Such an approach, it is hoped, will prove a convenience to the reader looking for information about some portion of Terence's work. Still, while there has inevitably been some repetition in such a method, it is also hoped that the study can easily be read as a whole.

A word is in order about the nature of Terentian studies. Continental scholars, especially those writing in German, have concentrated more energy on Terence than have their English-speaking colleagues. Their concern is, furthermore, typical of the scholarship on Terence in general in that it often focuses on technical questions, especially of a literary-historical nature. Terence's relation to Greek New Comedy, for example, is the single most studied facet of his work. The fruits of such scholarship will be seen in the present study, but its primary purpose is to present a literary and interpretative view of Terence's plays. Those interested in more technical questions will find ample sources for further reading in the selected bibliography.

Technical matters cannot be ignored altogether, however, especially as some must be confronted in order to gain an understanding of how we are to think of Terence's work in its own setting. Accordingly, the first two chapters contain discussions of such matters as his biography and his literary career, which are based often on an analysis of rather detailed evidence. Here, for example, one will find analyses of the plays' prologues, of the production notices associated with each play, and of the *Life of Terence* by Suetonius. The reader who wants only the "bottom line" in such questions will find appropriate summary sections. Students of classical literature will understand the need for a somewhat extended treatment of the poet's life, for biographical assumptions have had great influence on critical views of Terence as a playwright.

Finally, special thanks must be expressed to my colleague Professor Leon Golden, with whom I have had many profitable conversations about comedy in general and Terence in particular. I am also eager to acknowledge my debt to Mary Haskins, my wife, who has helped throughout this project in ways as varied as giving advice on questions of interpretation to proof-reading typescript.

Walter E. Forehand

Florida State University

Chronology

(All dates are B.C.)

254 Traditional date of birth of Plautus, Roman comic playwright.

240 Greek drama comes to Rome; Livius Andronicus active.

201 End of Second Punic War; Rome the greatest power in the Mediterranean.

195? Terence born in Africa.

185 Traditional date of Terence's birth; birth of Scipio Aemilianus, Roman statesman and perhaps Terence's patron.

184 Death of Plautus.

168 Death of Caecilius Statius, Roman comic playwright and perhaps patron of Terence.

166? First performance of *The Girl from Andros.*

165? First, unsuccessful performance of *The Mother-in-Law.*

163? First performance of *The Self-Tormentor.*

161? First performances of *The Eunuch* and *Phormio.*

160? Second, unsuccessful performance of *The Mother-in-Law;* first performance of *The Brothers;* third, successful performance of *The Mother-in-Law;* Terence leaves Rome for Greece.

159? Death of Terence in Greece.

Chapter One

Terence's Biography:
External Evidence

"Terence was a slave!" So the great French critic Denis Diderot began his "Praise of Terence" (ca. 1769). His is a romantic reaction to the first sentence of our principal source for the biography of Terence, the *Life of Terence* by Gaius Suetonius Tranquillus (ca. A.D. 69–after 130). His emotional outburst is typical of the effect this brief biographical sketch has had upon historical impressions of this Roman playwright.

In fact, though Suetonius's *Life,* preserved by the scholar-Aelius Donatus (fourth century A.D.), is our most complete source for Terence's life, we have two other sources from which we may derive information pertinent to a re-creation of his biography. One of these is a group of production notices, called *didascaliae,* which have come down to us in our manuscripts. The other is the prologues Terence himself wrote for each of his plays and in which he mentions many details regarding arguments concerning the writing and production of his works.

We might refer to Suetonius's *Life* and the *didascaliae* as the external evidence for Terence's biography. From them we can derive whatever is possible of the details of his life. The prologues are internal evidence. From these we can glean some understanding of his literary career. Accordingly, we will devote our attention in this first chapter to Terence's general biography and in the second to his life as a playwright. Such effort is necessary not because we know much about Terence, but because, in comparison to our knowledge of other ancient authors, we appear to know much, and reconstructions of our poet's life have had considerable influence on critical evaluations of his accomplishments.

Suetonius's *Life of Terence*

The *Life of Terence* was originally part of Suetonius's collection
of biographies, *On Poets,* from which several other lives have
survived, including those of Vergil (70–19 B.C.) and Horace
(65–8 B.C.). Donatus preserves it, along with a one-paragraph
addendum of his own, at the beginning of his commentary.
Even a casual reading of the *Life* reveals much disagreement
among the ancient authorities, so that critics in all ages have
seen that the material must be used with extreme care. Such
is our thirst for information of any sort about the ancient authors,
however, that few scholars have been willing to dismiss the
account out of hand.[1] Perhaps we should begin our investigation
with an uncritical précis of the essential details presented in
the *Life.*

Publius Terentius Afer was born in Carthage, lived between
the Second and Third Punic Wars (201–149 B.C.), and came
to Rome as the slave of a senator, Terentius Lucanus. Lucanus
educated and soon manumitted him, because of his talents and
good looks. Terence was of medium height, graceful build,
and dark complexion. He became friendly with powerful individuals, such as, possibly, Scipio Aemilianus (185/4–129 B.C.)
and Laelius (ca. 190–ca. 123 B.C.), who were attracted by his
mental and physical attributes. His first literary success came
with *The Girl from Andros* (*Andria*). He was asked to present
the play to the judgment of the old comic master Caecilius
Statius (d. 168 B.C.). Having been admitted to the old man
while he was at dinner, the young poet, dressed in tatters, com-
menced to read sitting on a stool, but made such an impression
with the first few lines that he was asked to join the company
at table. The reading proceeded after dinner to Caecilius's approval, and the young poet's career was launched. He presented
six plays: *The Girl from Andros, The Self-Tormentor* (*Heautontimo-
roumenos*), *The Eunuch* (*Eunuchus*), *Phormio* (*Phormio*), *The
Mother-in-Law* (*Hecyra*), and *The Brothers* (*Adelphoe*). *The Eunuch*
was an exceptional financial success. During his career he was
frequently accused of receiving help in his writing from Laelius
and Scipio, or other men of influence. After the staging of his
last comedy, he left Rome for a tour of Greece, "not yet having
entered his twenty-fifth year." During his stay there he wrote

a number of new plays. These were lost, probably in a shipwreck, while he was returning to Rome. The poet either met his fate with them, or survived only to die of a broken heart at their loss, or died of an illness in Greece. He left behind a daughter, who married a Roman knight.

Such is the simple core of the *Life.* Other material, including statements of a literary nature by such authorities as Cicero (106–43 B.C.) and Julius Caesar (100–44 B.C.), is interspersed throughout the account. These have considerable interest for a literary appraisal of Terence, but more germane to the present discussion are the many examples of disagreement among the ancient sources cited by Suetonius. The latter may have worked with one basic source for his life,[2] but clearly he consulted several other authorities as well and frequently records conflicting opinions. What is more, in the tradition of ancient biography, he presents much that seems more formulaic than credible, much that is anecdotal, and much that is raw gossip. Thus, if we are to arrive at a critical evaluation of the *Life,* as free as possible from prejudice and romantic embroidery, we must put into context the material in our short summary.

Terence's Dates.　The *Life* places Terence between the Second and Third Punic Wars (201–149 B.C.) and records that he left Rome for Greece "not yet having entered his twenty-fifth year." There is evidence outside the *Life* to place the production of his plays between 166 and 160 B.C. It is generally assumed that he died shortly after going to Greece; some authorities state flatly that he died in 159 B.C. Elsewhere in the *Life* we learn that some said he was the same age as Scipio Aemilianus (b. 185 or 184 B.C.). Thus, if 159 B.C. is taken as his year of death, if he was twenty-six at his death, and if he was the same age as Scipio, we have several reasons to fix 185 B.C. as his birth year.

That he was so young and died such an untimely death has given impetus to some quite romantic views of our poet. His first play would have been produced in his late teens. His reputation would have been thoroughly established by twenty-four. And the potential evidenced by such gifts was wasted by his premature death. Terence, then, must rank among the great precocious geniuses of Western letters, and must be mourned along with other talented artists sacrificed on the wheel of fortune. There are, however, difficulties with this scheme.

The ancient sources record no firm date for Terence's birth. Suetonius does quote some sources for a death date of 159 B.C. and gives us his age upon leaving Rome. There is a textual problem, however, in the passage recording that he left before his "twenty-fifth" year. Some manuscripts are garbled; some support the reading "thirty-fifth" year. Nor is there overwhelming reason to accept that the poet died in 159 B.C. Accounts of his trip to Greece varied. Some alleged that he went because of pressure from attacks on his reputation stemming from the rumor that influential friends were helping with his writing; others attributed the trip to whim, or said that he wanted to study Greek customs firsthand in order to improve his understanding of the Greek playwrights. Thus, we lose confidence in other details of the journey. Moreover, there is some textual evidence to support the astonishing information that he was starting back from Greece with 108 (!) plays adapted from Menander (342/1–291/0 B.C.). The text is uncertain, and most editors do not read the number 108 at this point, but simply "with plays adapted from Menander." If, however, the number 108 should be correct, or at least indicative of a large group of plays, Terence's work must have required an extended stay in Greece.

On literary grounds also one may hesitate over the dates 185–159 B.C. It is hard indeed to accept *The Girl from Andros* as the work of a teenage youth. In fact, in view of the uncertainty of the evidence, even if one accepts 159 B.C. as the year of Terence's death, 185 B.C. seems unlikely as his year of birth. We can think of Terence as young without ascribing to him such remarkable precocity.

This nexus of doubt has led many scholars to push back the date of Terence's birth to 195 B.C., usually by affording some weight to the reading "thirty-fifth year" of our manuscripts. Most hold to 159 B.C. for his death, so that one finds in recent works ca. 195–159 B.C. typically given as his dates.[3] Such a dating is based on a balanced appraisal of the evidence. If one should wish the most conservative statement, however, he may think of Terence as born in or before 185 B.C., dead in or after 159 B.C.

Nationality and Slave Status. Suetonius asserts in the first sentence of his *Life* that Terence was born in Carthage and came to Rome as a slave. Some thought he had been a prisoner of war, but others argued against this view on grounds that there had been no war during the period when he came to Rome. Furthermore, the name Afer, usually taken to indicate Terence's Carthaginian origins, was used in Latin to refer to North African in general, often to Libyan. Thus, neither ancient nor modern authorities have accepted at face value that Terence was from Carthage.

In fact, we cannot be sure that he was ever a slave. The name Afer, presumably taken by the young freedman as an indication of his origin, was occasionally used as a name independent of connection with Africa. It was a commonplace in the biographies of Roman playwrights to record that they began their careers as slaves; cf. Livius Andronicus (ca. 284–ca. 204 B.C.) and Caecilius Statius, both of whom were said to have been slaves. Thus, one may reasonably posit that reports of Terence's slave origins were slanderous or commonplaces of the biographer's trade. The fact that he bore the unusual name Afer provided a convenient place for his birth, and Carthage was the most famous African city of the day. Since freed slaves regularly assumed the family name of their former masters, a Terentius Lucanus was supplied to complete the story. Such a reconstruction is not widely accepted, but there is nothing in it to offend logic.[4]

Let us grant, however, that Terence was an African and a slave. None of our sources addresses what to us would seem a very interesting question, that is, how Terence came to be one of the premier Latin stylists of the second century.[5] Just as we marvel at the mastering of English style by a Conrad or a Nabokov, so we must be curious about how a foreign slave accomplished the considerable feat of acquiring native competence in Latin and, presumably, Greek, by age eighteen according to some accounts. The *Life* says that he was given a liberal education by his master and freed "soon" or "in good time." There is really nothing to preclude his coming to Rome as an infant. It has also been suggested that his family had come to Carthage from Greek-speaking Italy with slaves taken by Hannibal during the Second Punic War (218–201 B.C.), so that Greek and Latin may have been languages of the home.[6] Still, as interesting as the question may be, nothing in our biographical sources suggests an answer.

One final point concerning nationality has been raised by Suetonius's statement that Terence was "dark-complected" (Latin: *fuscus*). It has led to the view expressed from time to time that he was a black African.[7] As in the case of similar suggestions about Hannibal, one should note that regardless of whether Terence was of Carthaginian or Libyan descent, he would not have been from areas to the south and east, such as Ethiopia, from which black Africans usually came. *Fuscus* would fit well with a northeast African of Berber descent. Even more to the point, such physical descriptions have little foundation. A physical description was expected in the ancient biographies of artists and poets. The adjective *fuscus* may well have been suggested by the name *Afer*.

Terence's "Powerful Friends." The *Life* spends a good deal of time discussing the charge that Terence was assisted in writing his plays by certain men of influence in Rome—Terence himself referred to the charge in the prologues of *The Self-Tormentor* and *The Brothers*. Suetonius in fact quotes the passage from *The Brothers*. The names most frequently attached to these "powerful friends" were Scipio Aemilianus and Laelius, of whom, some also said, he was a favorite because of his good looks. Even in antiquity there was not clear agreement about either the validity of the charge or the identity of the friends.

Terence did not deny the association. In fact, he acknowledged it with pleasure, though this need not be taken as a plea of nolo contendere. His friends may have been flattered by the rumors, even if they had little to do with his plays. One authority, however, claimed to know on reliable evidence that Laelius had composed a portion of *The Self-Tormentor* (line 723, and perhaps those following) one evening on vacation at his villa near the Bay of Naples. And so, extremists implied that Terence was a sort of stooge whose name could be conveniently used as a cover for the literary pastimes of the upper class.

Yet, many doubted the truth of the charges and even more so the connection with Scipio and Laelius. They pointed out that had Terence wanted help in constructing his plays there were men available of greater reputation and greater literary accomplishment than Scipio and Laelius, who were just beginning their careers.

Despite the skepticism of ancient authorities, the connection with Scipio and Laelius is now widely accepted.[8] Certainly, it is supported by the tradition, but there are other circumstances that have inclined scholars to accept this view more readily than they might have from the evidence of the *Life* alone. During the middle of the second century B.C. Rome was undergoing a cultural transition that had become a political issue. One faction took a conservative approach to the changes at Rome, among them a growing interest in Greek art, literature, and philosophy. The other, the faction identified with the Scipio family and its allies, strongly supported the new movements. In more modern times the term Scipionic Circle has been used to refer to the philhellenic intellectual pursuits of Scipio, Laelius, and their friends. This invites a circular argument: Scipio and Laelius were linked with Terence in antiquity; they supported the arts; Terence was, therefore, one of the artists in their patronage; but in the other direction, Terence was associated with powerful men interested in literature; Scipio and Laelius supported the arts; therefore, Scipio and Laelius were those powerful friends.

The question can be resolved no further. We must take careful warning, however, of the pitfalls accompanying interpretations of Terence that make too much reference to quasi-political involvement in programs supported by the Scipionic faction. One can find support for positing such an involvement, but the evidence is by no means overwhelming.

Summary of Suetonius's *Life*.   In summary, then, we must assert the necessity for caution in dealing with Suetonius's *Life of Terence*. It is possible to question every piece of information in it to such an extent that nothing of value is left to us. Most scholars would stop short of dismissing the document completely, however, for enough information can be substantiated from other sources to suggest a thread of truth running through the web of gossip, literary formulae, and anecdote. We are left, at the very least, with a young man who rose to some considerable reputation as a playwright in the middle of the second century B.C., produced at least six plays based on Greek sources, achieved some financial success, and was associated with men of influence. He probably came to Rome as a slave from Africa and died while still young in Greece.

On the other hand, our real knowledge of Terence's biography is limited enough so that we should avoid too romantic assumptions about him. We should exercise restraint in the use of biographical criticism to interpret his works and should be wary of many commonly held views about his life.

So much for the life of Terence as a whole. We have, in addition to Suetonius's *Life,* another important source for biographical data, namely, the *didascaliae,* which have accompanied his plays in our manuscripts. These would, apparently, allow us to date his plays quite precisely. And yet, this information, too, must be approached with care. It is to these *didascaliae* that we will turn our attention now.

Chronology of the Plays: The *Didascaliae*

On the surface the ancient production notices, *didascaliae,* surviving for all the plays except *The Girl from Andros* (for which Donatus supplies an equivalent), would seem to make us better informed about the production history of Terence's plays than of those of any other ancient playwright. The *didascalia* of *The Self-Tormentor* will serve as an example of the genre:

Here begins *The Self-Tormentor* of Terence. It was performed at the Games for the Great Mother [*Ludi Megalenses*] in the curule aedileship of Lucius Cornelius Lentulus and Lucius Valerius Flaccus. Lucius Ambivius Turpio and Lucius Atilius Praenestinus played the leading roles. Flaccus, slave of Claudius, made the music. In the first performance it was played with unequal pipes, later with two right-handed pipes. The Greek play was by Menander. It was the third, written in the consulship of Manius Iuventius and Tiberius Sempronius.

This short notice gives us a wealth of data: the author of the Greek original, the principal actors, the aediles responsible for the games at which the play was first presented, the composer-performer of the musical accompaniment, even the instrument on which he performed, the date of the performance (163 B.C., the year of these consuls, in April, when the games in honor of the Great Mother were held), and the order of this piece in the Terentian corpus. We must return to this *didascalia* in a moment. For now we can summarize uncritically the information presented by the *didascaliae* as a group.

The team of Ambivius Turpio and Atilius Praenestinus acted in all of Terence's plays except *The Mother-in-Law,* in which Ambivius Turpio and Sergius Turpio played the principal roles. The slave Flaccus handled the music for all the plays. Terence presented plays four times at the Games for the Great Mother (*Ludi Megalenses*), held in April, including the first performance of *The Mother-in-Law. Phormio* and the third *The Mother-in-Law* were presented at the Roman Games (*Ludi Romani*), held in September. *The Brothers* and the second *The Mother-in-Law* were given at special games as part of the funeral celebration for Lucius Aemilius Paullus. Four of the plays were adapted from Greek plays by Menander. *The Mother-in-Law* and *Phormio* were based on plays by Apollodorus of Carystus (fl. 285 B.C.), a close follower of Menander.[9] The plays are dated as follows: *The Girl from Andros* (April 166 B.C.); first *The Mother-in-Law* (April 165 B.C.); *The Self-Tormentor* (April 163 B.C.); *The Eunuch* and *Phormio* (April and September 161 B.C.); second *The Mother-in-Law* and *The Brothers* (at the same funeral games in 160 B.C.); third *The Mother-in-Law* (September 160 B.C.).

Now, as the *didascaliae* stand there are minor problems. Some of these are textual; others arise from inconsistencies. These must be corrected or explained in order to preserve the scheme we have presented. As an example, let us turn again to the *didascalia* of *The Self-Tormentor.* The manuscripts differ on the reading of the number indicating where the play stood in the Terentian corpus. Thus, some editors read "it was written third"; others, "it was written second." One can argue either reading and preserve our order: composed third, second successful production, because of the debacle of *The Mother-in-Law.* What are we to make, however, of the statement that at the first performance the unequal pipes were used, while later two right-hand pipes were played? The usual explanation, that the *didascalia* is giving information both about the first production and a second one occurring after Terence's death,[10] may be accurate, but it is clearly speculative. Other *didascaliae* exhibit similar problems.[11]

These problems are minor taken by themselves, but there

is a more troublesome difficulty. It is hard to reconcile what the prologues tell us about Terence's career with the chronology dictated by the *didascaliae*. Why, for example, in the third prologue of *The Mother-in-Law* does Ambivius Turpio imply that he continued to put on the plays of Caecilius Statius until they succeeded (18–22) and proposed to handle Terence's play similarly, if the first failure occurred in 165 and second and third attempts were not made until 160 B.C.? Why, in fact, are there two *didascaliae* for *The Mother-in-Law?* Why does the prologue of *The Brothers* caution the audience not to expect an expository prologue (22–24)? Several plays make reference to Terence's unique form of prologue, but surely those that do so were presented earliest in his career. Yet the *didascalia* records that *The Brothers* was his last play. In short, much explanation is needed to demonstrate that the prologues follow reasonably the chronology derived from the *didascaliae*.

This is not the time for a complete discussion of Terence's prologues, which provide us with many hints about the literary scene in Terence's Rome and his place in it. To complete our analysis of the chronology of his plays, however, it will be necessary to refer to some degree to their contents.

Since the *didascaliae* are so replete with problems of interpretation, it is not surprising that some scholars have dissented from the standard view of the order of Terence's plays, and have also suggested that other plays besides *The Mother-in-Law* may have been presented more than once.[12] No alternative has gained general acceptance. One, however, that of H. Mattingly, is based on arguments that are of special interest to a construction of Terence's career. It has also gained some acceptance,[13] so that it deserves to be presented in some length.

In Mattingly's view the *didascaliae* are sufficiently flawed so as to undermine our confidence in them. Thus, in an effort to provide a fresh perspective on the question of Terentian chronology, he constructs an order of the plays based on the evidence of the prologues. His order is *The Girl from Andros; The Self-Tormentor* and *The Brothers* (without strong conviction as to which of these two was first); the three performances of *The Mother-in-Law* (all within a relatively brief span); *Phormio; The Eunuch.* The prologues of the first three deal with related questions while those of the last three move on to other issues.

The first group talks of Terence's new style of prologue, the slanders directed at his relationship to his powerful friends, and the argument over "ruining" plays. In the second group there is an emphasis on arguments over style, with Terence becoming increasingly more specific in his counterattacks against his critics, and a careful acknowledgment of the actor's importance to a successful performance, a preoccupation, one supposes, arising from Ambivius Turpio's energetic work on behalf of *The Mother-in-Law*.

Thus, the scheme suggested by Mattingly helps us to follow the flow of Terence's career more easily than does the traditional chronology. In his early, tentative days he took criticism from Luscius Lanuvinus and the establishment about "ruining" plays to heart. After *The Girl from Andros* he presented *The Self-Tormentor,* adapted from only one Greek original, and *The Brothers,* containing its scene from a play by Diphilus omitted by Plautus when he adapted the play, so that this play presented a sort of textbook case to expose the close-minded attitude of the establishment toward the use of Greek materials. The young playwright was nervous enough about his second play to call on Ambivius Turpio to deliver the prologue of *The Self-Tormentor* personally. He was also beset in this period with slanderous rumors about his relationship to his friends. *The Mother-in-Law* marked the watershed of his career. His success had given him the confidence to attempt a quiet, philosophical play. Its problems in the theater, even if they were created by the underhanded tactics of his enemies, shook Terence, and he was very grateful to Ambivius Turpio for his support. He began to launch direct criticism of his own instead of making cryptic allusions to his rival's deficiencies as he had done in earlier prologues. Luscius Lanuvinus may even have retired from writing at about the time of *Phormio*.[14] When *The Eunuch* achieved its great success, Terence's reputation was secure, and he could contemplate the trip to Greece reported in the *Life*.

We must remember that this view has not received the endorsement of the scholarly community at large. Nonetheless, most scholars warn against interpretations of Terence's work that assume as gospel a fixed chronology in which his talents as a playwright developed. If we should accept Mattingly's order for the plays, what happens to our dating? Since the *didascaliae* provide our principal mileposts for the dates of Terence's life, we are left with very little. Some ancient authorities did record his death as occurring in 159 B.C., but we have seen already that the evidence does not compel us to accept this as fact. The tradition does generally agree that Terence was young when he began his career and that he died young. It also places his life in the first half of the second century. Beyond these limits we are left with only a relative order for the plays and a few inferences. If Terence died young and his prologues all deal with controversies appropriate to a beginning playwright, the plays were probably written within a reasonably short time. In fact, Mattingly's scheme is not at variance with a literary career of 166 to 160 B.C., the traditional *floruit* period, but it does not require it.

In the final analysis, we need not abandon all the traditional views about Terence. There is no reason to feel uncomfortable with a life span from ca. 195 to ca. 159 B.C. and a literary career covering ca. 166 to ca. 160 B.C. We may accept, with caution, the claim that he wrote six plays only (excepting those he was to bring back from Greece). We should, however, remain cautious about the order of his plays, and so about critical appraisals that rely heavily on assumptions based on his biography or his poetic development.

Chapter Two
Terence's Literary Career

The comedies of Terence begin with an unusual kind of prologue. The usual practice of the comic playwrights was to provide an introduction delivered by one of the actors in which information was given about the play to follow. Terence, however, wrote a different sort of prologue, a type he may have invented, in which he dealt not with the contents of the play but with criticisms of his work made by the theatrical establishment at Rome. Thus, these prologues are a rich source of information about the brief literary career of our playwright and give us interesting insights into the theatrical practices and theories of his day. Valuable as they are, however, they are fraught with many difficulties of interpretation.

First of all, Terence's prologues often share in common with any document treating contemporary issues the disadvantage (from the perspective of later generations) of being cryptic. Specific allusions, technical vocabulary, and discussions of subjects begun in midstream often leave us only vaguely in control of Terence's meaning. Second, the chronological order of the plays, a consideration that must greatly affect our appraisal of the information in the prologues, is a matter of debate, as we found in our discussion of the *didascaliae* in chapter 1. And, as we heard there, much of the debate over chronology has centered on the reliability of information found in the prologues.

Despite these very real problems, the prologues offer us our best view of Terence and his literary world so that we must examine them in detail in order to complete the bibliographical study begun in chapter 1. We will treat the plays in the traditional order, but remembering while so doing the warnings about a too uncritical acceptance of that order.

Terence's Prologues

The Girl from Andros. There is general agreement that
The Girl from Andros is the earliest of Terence's plays. Its prologue is short and will serve as an example of Terence's form,
so that we can profitably present its text in toto.

When the poet first turned his attention to writing he thought his
sole concern was that the plays he had constructed please the people.
But he learns that matters turn out much differently, for he wastes
his efforts on writing prologues, not to relate the plot, but to answer
the slanders of a malevolent old poet. Now, please pay attention to
what they claim to be a flaw. Menander wrote *The Girl from Andros*
and *The Girl from Perinthos.* Whoever is well acquainted with either
knows them both. They are not very different in plot. Still, they have
been written with different dialogues and in a different style. He admits
that he has transferred from *The Girl from Andros* those parts which
were appropriate and has used them for his own purposes. Those
detractors find fault with this procedure, and they contend that it is
not proper for plays to be ruined in this way. Do they show by their
knowledge that they know nothing? When they accuse him, they accuse
Naevius [ca. 270–ca. 241 B.C.], Plautus [254?–184 B.C.], and Ennius
[239–169 B.C.], whom our poet has as authorities and whose carelessness he would much rather follow than the crabbed carefulness of
these detractors. Furthermore, I warn them to hold their peace hence-
forth and stop their slanders, so they do not find out their own misfea-
sances. Show good will, be fair-minded, and watch the production,
so that you may know what hope, if any, remains for the future,
whether you should see the comedies he will write anew hereafter
or drive them away before they are played. (1–27)[1]

As we have warned, several items in the text are quite unclear.
Who is the "old poet"? Who are the "detractors"? What is
wrong with the procedure Terence has followed? What is meant
by "carelessness" and "crabbed carefulness," if, in fact, these
are adequate translations? Few of these questions can be definitively resolved, but we can shed some light upon them.
  The very existence of this prologue raises an interesting question. If the play was Terence's first, why should he need to
defend himself against criticism? Several explanations suggest
themselves. Perhaps in some way Terence had become aware
of criticism even before his play was performed. It may have

been seen in rehearsal—we know from the prologue of *The Eunuch* that "dress" rehearsals were sometimes given for the officials in charge of the festival at which a play was to be presented. The old poet, identified by Donatus as one Luscius Lanuvinus, about whom we know practically nothing except what we learn from these prologues, could have seen the rehearsal and started his campaign of criticism before the play opened, prompting Terence's prologue. Just as likely, the play may have circulated in manuscript around Rome's theatrical community with similar results.

It is also possible, however, that *The Girl from Andros* had been seen by the public already, either as part of an earlier, unsuccessful performance or as a play successful enough to gain a repeat performance.[2] We know from the problems associated with *The Mother-in-Law,* presented twice without being acted to completion before its successful performance, that plays did not always run to conclusion. We have hints of repeat performances, for example, in the case of *The Eunuch,* though the text of the *Life* that records this is problematic. Or, perhaps Terence had already tried his hand at other plays that had not gained a successful hearing so that he was familiar with a line of criticism of his work.

Speculative though such ideas may be, they should be pursued a bit further. In the prologue Terence speaks of pleasing the audience with plays (plural) and of wasting his time writing prologues (plural). Now, such a loose use of the rhetorical plural need imply nothing at all about the existence of other plays, but it would be compatible with some dramatic activity before the successful production of *The Girl from Andros.* Without arguing that such a view should be adopted—surely, most scholars would not accept the premise—we should note nonetheless that such an apprenticeship would help to account for the high quality of *The Girl from Andros.* It is the work of a talented artist in control of his craft, and even precocity and genius do not completely explain how Terence mastered such technique.

Let us return to the prologue proper. We can glean valuable information about Terence's career. Clearly, Terence was embroiled in a quarrel with literary enemies, led by the "old poet," and we have no reason to doubt that he was Luscius Lanuvinus. The issue was over some sort of supposed impropriety in dramatic usage, centering on the use of material from two plays of Menander in a single Latin play. Somehow that procedure "ruined" plays (the Latin word is *contaminare*). We do not understand exactly what theories of composition were violated.[3] Other prologues address similar charges so that we may feel sure that Terence's methods were at odds with the dictates of the poetic establishment. These rules probably arose from general agreement of the members of the Roman guild in which playwrights enrolled and not from actual legislation, although they amount to a rough form of copyright protection.[4] Now, Terence did not belong to the guild, or so it would seem. His poetic theories were innovative, and his stance as a maverick posed a potential threat to the poets of the guild. Hence, he was criticized, especially by Luscius Lanuvinus, and defended himself by making a virtue of his supposed fault, trying in the process to establish a pedigree for his methods.

The Self-Tormentor.   Whereas the prologue of *The Girl from Andros* was delivered in the guise of the playwright addressing his audience, using the third person basically but on one occasion slipping into the first person, the introductory remarks of *The Self-Tormentor* are spoken in the person of a veteran actor, who stands forth as an advocate for the young poet. He can be identified as Lucius Ambivius Turpio, the head of an important acting troupe and a leading force in Terence's career. In fact, he cleverly establishes his position through a pun on the Latin *actor,* "one who pleads a case," or "play actor": "He [the poet] wanted me to deliver a speech, not a prologue. He has made you the judges, me the pleader (*actor*). But will this player (*actor*) have as much eloquence as the one who wrote this speech that I'll deliver has ability to express himself?" (11–15).

Ambivius Turpio's appearance is significant on two counts. First, it indicates the extent to which Terence was well placed. His plays were handled by an established, successful actor-producer. Second, one must wonder what pressures from his detractors were sufficiently great to cause the young playwright to call upon Ambivius Turpio's personal authority. Terence apparently felt the sting of his critics, and he may have been concerned over the problems connected with his production of *The Mother-*

in-Law, which did not receive a favorable initial reception. At any rate, his career seemed in enough jeopardy that he felt he needed as much support as possible to insure the success of *The Self-Tormentor.* The principal issue with which this prologue deals is the charge that Terence "ruined" plays. *The Self-Tormentor,* we are told immediately (4–6), has been adapted from a single Greek play, albeit the plot has been modified. Apparently, however, accusations persisted that the poet "has ruined many Greek plays while he makes a few Latin ones" (16–17). The prologue offers no defense, admitting instead that the poet has done what his critics said, but asserting that the procedure is not reprehensible, but founded on good precedent. In short, it repeats the basic line of argument in *The Girl from Andros.*

As in the prologue of that play, we find here a curious plural, i.e., his accusers speak of Terence's adulterating many Greek plays. Of course, this may be simple rhetorical hyperbole, on the part of either Terence or his critics, but he does not contradict them. Of the plays that might have preceded *The Self-Tormentor, The Girl from Andros* used two Greek models, hardly enough to classify as "many"; *The Brothers,* to which few would allow such an early date, used only one scene, from a second play, and that a work already adapted by Plautus. Consequently, we must consider the possibility that Terence wrote other, unsuccessful plays known to his critics but lost to us.[5]

One additional point is raised that relates to the Terentian biography. Ambivius Turpio acknowledges the old poet's charge that Terence had taken up playwriting all of a sudden, relying on the talent of his friends instead of his own gifts (22–24). As with the other charges, the poet offers no refutation, but merely asks the audience to judge his merits for themselves, a common ploy known as *captatio benevolentiae,* or a play for the audience's sympathy.

As we have seen from our discussion of the *Life,* this charge persisted throughout Terence's career. The evidence remains unclear as to the relationship of his friends to his plays, or as to who those friends were. Those who accept that they were Scipio and Laelius will find nothing in this passage to bolster their case.

After these comments, Ambivius Turpio, as Terence's advocate, turns to a discussion of the type of play the audience should expect from *The Self-Tormentor*. He bemoans the current practices calling for considerable wild action on the stage and alerts the audience that the upcoming play will rely heavily on purity of dialogue. Thus, we have confirmation of Terence's efforts to develop an individual style even against the popular practices of his day.

The Eunuch.   The prologue of *The Eunuch* is concerned almost wholly with the problem of "ruining" plays. As in the prologue of *The Girl from Andros,* the argument centers around the acceptable procedures, the "rules of the game," for using material from the Greek stage in Roman plays. Terence tells us that the old poet interrupted the dress rehearsal of *The Eunuch,* calling Terence a thief because he had taken material from a Greek play already used in a Latin adaptation, in fact used by both Naevius and Plautus. Thus, Terence was guilty of a sort of plagiarism or de facto copyright violation.

Terence begins his defense with an attack, accusing Luscius Lanuvinus of clumsily handling a scene from Menander in such a way that it became absurd to a Roman audience. This is an example of his opponent's general failing: "he has produced not so good Latin plays out of good Greek ones by translating them well but composing them badly" (7–8). We recall that in the prologue of *The Girl from Andros* Terence spoke of his detractors as advocating a "crabbed carefulness," that is, a reliance on literal fidelity at the expense of dramatic verities.

He then turns to a formal explanation of his actions, but instead of a refutation of the charges we find a statement of literary theory. He admits that he did take characters from the play in question for use in *The Eunuch,* but denies any intent to violate the rules, pleading ignorance of the existence of the earlier plays. He tries to undercut his critics' position by calling attention to the wide use in comedy of generalized types, "stock" characters, and he implies that if the stringent rules of his pedantic detractors are carried to their logical conclusion, playwrights would be put out of business, for all their types have been anticipated already in the works of earlier poets.

The defense partakes more of rhetoric than reason, but it interests us on two counts. We see in it the extent to which

Terence was willfully in conflict with an establishment view of play construction. He may not, in fact, have known of the two earlier plays, since even a professional in the mid-second century might be forgiven for not having read the many, many plays that had been produced before his day. But that is not really the point: he is arguing for freedom in composition against the constraints the establishment would have liked to have placed upon the theater. Second, we can detect a spirit of confidence in Terence that he has gained a toehold from which he can withstand his enemies without capitulation. If we can trust the *Life, The Eunuch* was a notable financial success.

Phormio.   The prologue of *Phormio* reveals little that has not become familiar to us from the plays with which we have dealt already. Certain features are, however, worth noting. Terence accuses the old poet, Luscius Lanuvinus, of attempting to force him literally from the practice of poetry, and he places the responsibility for the quarrel, as usual, squarely on the other side: "That man [the old poet] intended to drive our poet from the profession into starvation. Our poet wished merely to respond, not to injure. Had he made his criticism in friendly words, he would have heard like ones in return" (18–20).

In the process of delivering his short message, Terence's prologue raises two interesting issues. First, he answers the charge that his writing exhibited "thin dialogue and weak writing" (line 5) by holding up to ridicule a scene from one of his antagonist's recent plays. Luscius Lanuvinus's barb had struck home. His opponents had perceived and criticized an aspect of Terence's inventive style that later generations would also question. He ran the risk of losing comic power, what Caesar called *vis comica* in a poem quoted in the *Life,* while writing quieter, more elevated plays than those commonly seen on the Roman stage.

Second, near the end of his prologue Terence feels the need to make reference to a dramatic failure, which doubtless also rankled him. He ends with a *captatio benevolentiae* in which he calls for the audience's kind attention so that his play may have no fear of suffering the same fate as its predecessor "when our company was forced from the stage by an uproar" (line 31). Although most scholars assume that the reference is to the unsuc-

cessful first attempt to produce *The Mother-in-Law,* it is possible
that some other failure is meant, and the passage thus lends
some support to the theory that our extant plays do not represent
Terence's entire dramatic effort, only his successful plays. Under
any circumstances, we find here a clear admission of the uncertain route of Terence's road to success.

The Mother-in-Law.   In *The Mother-in-Law* we find an
unusual situation in that the play has two prologues, one for
its second production, another for its third, occasioned by two
abortive performances at which the play was not completed.
These prologues, especially the second, are fascinating documents, for they give us our fullest firsthand account of production practices of the Roman stage in the time of Terence, albeit
one tinged with partisan rhetoric. In addition, they provide information about the fate of *The Mother-in-Law,* an important chapter
in Terence's career.

There are vague hints in the *Life* of problems with *The Mother-
in-Law.* Suetonius writes, "He gained popular approval for this
play [*The Eunuch*] and the five remaining ones, although Volcacius in his enumeration of them writes thusly. . . ." We omit
Volcacius's comment to avoid a misleading translation, for the
text is uncertain. The general tenor seems to have been that
The Mother-in-Law would be or had been left out, of what or
why remains unclear. Donatus in his short addendum to the
Life says, "*The Mother-in-Law* is often excluded; it is scarcely
acted [or, perhaps, 'acted with difficulty,' the Latin adverb is
vix]." Again, the meaning of this is unclear, but the implication
surely is that *The Mother-in-Law* was not as successful as the
other plays.[6]

Before considering the two extant prologues, we should mention the prologue of the first production, that is, the one that
has not survived. In fact, there is no evidence that such a prologue ever existed.[7] If there was no prologue, then *The Mother-
in-Law* is alone among the surviving plays. And, if there is a
precedent for the omission of the prologue entirely, one might
use this datum to support, for example, an unrecorded first
performance of *The Girl from Andros* played without a prologue.

The first extant prologue is quite brief. It outlines the debacle
of the first production. On that occasion a tumult caused by a

preoccupation with a tightrope walker forced a halt to the performance. Beyond this there is only the curious comment that the play should be considered new, but not just so that it can be sold a second time. We would like to understand this comment better. Does the term "new" simply mean that the play was really never seen before, or does it imply major revisions of the previous version? What exactly is meant by reselling the play? On this point we have at least some information from other sources: apparently plays were sold both directly to producers, such as Ambivius Turpio, and to magistrates in charge of public games, who in turn offered them to producers. However, a play which was not performed might revert back to the author, and so intentional failures might have been engineered to increase revenues from a piece.[8] Thus, Terence may be simply assuring his audience that he acts in the interest of art, not commerce.

The second, much longer prologue is more informative. We learn from it that the play failed again on its second attempt, and so Ambivius Turpio stepped forth, as he does in *The Self-Tormentor,* to plead the playwright's case personally. His defense is divided into three parts: a recitation of his experiences with Caecilius Statius when the old master was a struggling young writer, a recapitulation of the problems encountered by the two previous attempts to produce *The Mother-in-Law,* and a *captatio benevolentiae* to the audience, asking for a hearing to counteract the efforts of the young poet's enemies to ruin his career.

The first section forges a link between Terence and Caecilius Statius through Ambivius Turpio's involvement in the careers of both. That a playwright of Caecilius Statius's stature should have had so much difficulty in his early career is a strong indication of the vicissitudes of the Roman stage. We must remember this when we question the power of Terence's play to hold its audience. The connection between the two also recalls the story in Suetonius's *Life* of Terence's visit to the old poet to gain approval for his first play. If the incident was real, the involvement with Ambivius Turpio would account for the unknown poet's access to the established dean of the playwrights. On the other hand, this passage may have been the inspiration for concocting the anecdote that appears in the *Life.*

After his lesson in theatrical history, Ambivius Turpio addresses the play's previous failures. On the first occasion he had just begun to act when the approach of some boxers and the hubbub of their accompanying retinue caused an uproar, increased also by the murmur of a rumor that a tightrope act was imminent. The confusion forced the performance to stop. At the second attempt the play went well during the first part, but a rumor that a gladiatorial show was soon to take place caused an onrush of people trying to push their way into the theater. Again the performance was disrupted.

We have no reason to doubt that Ambivius Turpio's accounts are substantially correct, even though he does augment what we are told in the first prologue about the first performance. But can we say anything further about this bad luck? Terence has been criticized in both ancient and modern times for lacking a flare for robust comedy, and for falling into a too intellectual style. The failures of *The Mother-in-Law* have often been cited to prove that his contemporary audiences also found him dull. *The Mother-in-Law* is, in fact, a rather quiet, thoughtful play; however, its problems may well have had more to do with the tactics of Terence's enemies than with the vacillating attentions of a restless audience.

Certainly, Roman audiences were attracted by the excitement of tightrope walkers and gladiators. Gladiatorial combats were still unusual in the mid-second century B.C. Little doubt that the mere rumor of a show sent people pushing and shoving into the theater, where such events were frequently held, despite the fact that a play was in progress. Both the performances were ultimately stopped by the noise and tumult of outside events, and few plays, regardless of their comic verve, could have survived such opposition. Caecilius Statius had to contend with many obstacles of this sort. What is more, one must wonder, even at this distance from the events, whether the bad luck that dogged the play did not get some of its impetus from Terence's literary opponents. Their tactics had included slander in addition to professional criticism. Why not subversion as well? Boxers could be sent down the street at the proper moment and rumors started. Terence complains that his enemies sought to drive him literally from the profession. Apparently the Roman stage in this period was a rough-and-tumble place.[9]

The Brothers.   The short prologue of *The Brothers* deals
with two issues for which we have had much preparation. The
first is the old question of "ruining" plays. Terence openly acknowledged that he used a scene from a play by Diphilus (before
340–after 289 B.C.), which had previously been presented by
Plautus. He was at pains to point out, however, that Plautus
had omitted the specific scene he was using, thus forestalling,
he hoped, charges of improperly using material already under
"copyright." In fact, Terence may have been constructing a
test case by which to answer his critics.[10] When was material
in control of an author, and when was it in the public domain?
The technicalities raised by adapting a fresh scene from a play
already claimed brought into focus the very niggling attitudes
toward composition to which Terence objected in the establishment view.

The second part of the prologue addresses the nagging criticism that Terence received help in the composition of his plays.
The passage is his longest statement on the subject and deserves
to be quoted here, as Suetonius did in the *Life:*

Now the charge which those malevolent detractors lodge, that eminent
men are helping the poet and continually write in consort with him,
a charge which they think the most grievous damnation, the poet
considers very great praise, since he wins favor with those whom all
you and the people at large favor, and upon whose efforts everyone
calls without being proud at important moments in war, in peace,
and in their own affairs. (15–21)

Obviously, Terence addresses the charge with no more direct-
ness here than he does in *The Self-Tormentor.* Rather, he plays
on the notoriety gained from such a rumor. Nor are we really
any closer to identifying the individuals involved. The fulsome
language used to describe his friends may be simple hyperbole,
but if it is to be taken literally, it argues against their being
Scipio and Laelius, whose reputations could not have been so
well developed at any time during Terence's literary career.
Still, the rumor was not stopped in antiquity. Suetonius remarks
with regard to this passage, "Moreover, he seems to have defended himself rather lightly, because he knew that this popular
opinion was not unpleasing to Laelius and Scipio, and it gained
strength into later times."

Summary of Terence's Literary Career

What, then, do the prologues add to our information about Terence and his career? Only two points may be made with confidence, one not mentioned in the *Life,* the other well-discussed there. First, Terence's literary career was embroiled in controversy with the dramatic establishment of his day, represented by an old playwright, Luscius Lanuvinus. If the prologues, partisan as they are, carry any objective account of the quarrel, it took the form of criticism and accusation against Terence on technical grounds regarding both his style and method of adapting Greek plays, for he was accused of violating the playwright's code for dealing with material from the Greek stage. Second, his opponents also resorted to slander, and perhaps even to underhanded subversion. At least we know that *The Mother-in-Law* was disrupted twice before receiving a complete hearing.

The slanders took the form of rumors that Terence had powerful connections who helped in the composition of his plays. Suetonius discusses this issue at length. Terence mentions it directly in the prologues of *The Self-Tormentor* and *The Brothers.* Terence never contradicts the rumor and, in fact, seems rather pleased at being placed in such company. There is nothing in his comments with which to identify these influential Romans, despite the statements in Suetonius's *Life* that they were Scipio Aemilianus and Laelius. Some ancients and moderns have disqualified them on evidence of the prologue to *The Brothers.* Finally, one might see a connection between such an involvement and Terence's feud with the literary establishment. That Terence was so well placed might have been viewed as an unfair advantage over other, guild poets, so that he had to be opposed for the sake of business. Or the attacks may have been politically motivated with the poets acting against one of their number allied with important men of repugnant political views. All such analysis must, however, remain pure speculation.

One of the more interesting stories told of Terence in the *Life* is of his visit to Caecilius Statius. Many scholars have doubted the incident, both because of factual matters concerning the date of Caecilius Statius's death and the beginning of Terence's career and because of the anecdotal quality of the account.

In the second prologue of *The Mother-in-Law* Ambivius Turpio links Terence's career with that of Caecilius Statius. Thus, on the one hand, the passage can be seen as evidence to support the story; on the other, it is the inspiration for the anecdote.

Replete as they are with problems for the literary historian and the student of Terence alike, the prologues remain our most direct link with the poet. Unlike other biographical evidence, they come from his own hand so that we must consider them carefully when we seek to reconstruct the details of his career on the Roman stage.

Chapter Three

Terence and the Theater of His Time

Terence did not work in a vacuum, nor did he invent the genre in which he wrote. In fact, he stands rather nearer the end than the beginning of the comic tradition that began at least three centuries earlier in Greece, came to Rome from the Greek world, and remained on the Roman stage for perhaps a hundred years thereafter, although the last fifty saw more revivals of old favorites than introductions of new plays.

Drama stood near the beginning of Roman letters. The nature of Roman society was such that creative literature came to it late. The Romans rarely used writing for anything more literary than laws, accounts, and religious incantations before the middle of the third century, by which time they had already become the leading power in the western Mediterranean. By tradition Roman letters began with Livius Andronicus (ca. 284–ca. 204 B.C.), who came to Rome in 242 as a slave from the southern Italian city of Tarentum, then heavily Grecized. He is credited with introducing epic into the Latin language through a translation, or paraphrase, of Homer's *Odyssey,* and with producing the first Latin tragedies and comedies from Greek models.

Public performances of a dramatic nature were not unknown to the Italians. For example, dancers were often depicted in Etruscan tombs giving evidence of trained performers in north-central Italy from early times. There was also a kind of comic contest popular at festivals in which, apparently, one performer tried to outdo an opponent with witticisms or humorous insults. Known as Fescennine Verses, these were delivered in an accentual meter called the Saturnian, developed in the Italic dialects and used by Livius Andronicus in his *Odyssia.* There were also farcical pieces, the Atellane plays, popular among Rome's near neighbors, the Oscans. These used stylized, standard characters much like a Punch and Judy show. Though the name of an occasional writer of Atellanes has been recorded, it was not a developed literary tradition.[1]

If, then, Rome did not develop a native literary drama, still there was an established tradition of scenic entertainment. The expansion of Roman political and military influence throughout southern Italy and Sicily brought more and more of her citizenry into contact with the Greek culture of those areas, where the well-developed conventions of the Greek stage were preserved. Greek culture had a profound influence on Rome in many areas: Roman religion, even in historical times more animistic than anthropomorphic, had been fundamentally modified by adopting the interesting and lively pantheon of the Greeks; the plastic arts fell heavily under the influence of Greek models; and so, by the mid-third century B.C. the Roman public was calling for plays in the Greek fashion to replace their more rustic fare.

The Greek Comic Tradition

The presentation of comic performances at religious festivals had its official beginning in Athens at the Lenaea, a celebration honoring the wine-god Dionysus, in 486 B.C. Comedy had a rich history throughout the fifth century B.C. in Athens.[2] The names of many writers and many fragments of their works have survived. Of this entire theater, however, complete plays are extant for only one playwright, Aristophanes (ca. 450–ca. 385 B.C.).

Still, from Aristophanes, from the fragments, and from the testimony of many ancient sources we know that these plays, usually referred to as Old Comedy, were raucous and vulgar in tone, fantastic and episodic in structure. They pilloried and satirized contemporary persons and made comic capital of current events. The general effect was accentuated by a gaily costumed chorus, which sang lyrical passages and danced to musical accompaniment.

This style gave way, however, about the end of the fifth century B.C. to a new form, called Middle Comedy. The cause of this transition is complex, but changes in the political atmosphere following the defeat of Athens in the Peloponnesian War (404 B.C.) did much to move comedy away from the personal attacks of the old style. What followed was a medium that dealt more with generalities and abstractions than with individuals and specific events. Again, we have names and fragments from this phase, which lasted until around 320 B.C. In addition, the last two plays of Aristophanes (*Women in Parliament* and *Wealth*) are from this time and fit well enough with what we know of the tradition generally so that they are usually classified as middle comedies. As the form developed, playwrights became more and more interested in depicting characters from daily life than in creating the spritely caricatures and inventions of Old Comedy. Furthermore, the episodic quality of Old Comedy gave way to a more coherent plot structure, and the lyrical and musical elements were much decreased.

Comedy continued to develop in Athens, so that Middle Comedy also changed. The traditional chorus was so diminished in importance that it ceased to be an integral part of the play and either took the form of a musical interlude or was omitted altogether. Middle Comedy with its emphasis on true-to-life characters and its generalized themes evolved into a comedy of manners exhibiting a fully developed set of stock characters and situations manipulated by the playwrights in various combinations and subtle ways. This form, called New Comedy, lasted perhaps until the middle of the third century B.C.

As with Old and Middle Comedy, New Comedy has left us names of authors, titles of plays, and numerous fragments. The only extant plays, however, are by Menander. One, *The Ill-Tempered Man* (*The Dyscolos*), survives virtually intact. Four others have enough remaining so that we can construct the plot lines with ease and understand the characters. In antiquity Menander was acknowledged as the king of this genre. Diphilus (before 340–after 289 B.C.) and Philemon (368/60–267/63 B.C.) were also well respected. Apollodorus of Carystus (fl. 285 B.C.), a close follower of Menander, is also of interest because of his influence on Terence.

The Dramatic Tradition at Rome

Ludi scaenici, "stage games," joined *ludi circenses,* "circus games," at the festivities of religious celebrations in Rome in 364 B.C. Thus, as in Athens, scenic performances had an official position in Roman society, and one that was well established long before Greek drama came to Rome. By the early second century B.C. there was ample opportunity for playwright and actor to ply their trades at several public festivals and in private celebrations.[3]

Four types of "legitimate" theater had developed by 200 B.C.[4] One was tragedy, based heavily on models from the fifth century B.C. Athenian stage, which were adapted to the tastes and language of a Roman audience. Many fragments survive, though we cannot reconstruct a complete play. Some of the practitioners of the art became respected names in the history of Roman literature. This genre continued hand in hand with other dramatic forms into the middle of the first century B.C., when "legitimate" theater began to yield the stage to farcical mimes and pantomimes, often of scurrilous content. The tradition continued among the educated, for men of affairs such as Cicero or Augustus Caesar (63 B.C.–A.D. 14) often tried their hands at tragedy. Such plays were not staged publicly. Only those of the politician and philosopher Seneca (ca. 5 B.C.–A.D. 65) have survived. These have been very influential in the history of Western drama.

Another form, again surviving only in fragments, was the *fabula praetexta,* so named for the *toga praetexta,* a garment trimmed in purple worn by Roman magistrates. This genre was apparently invented by the Roman playwright Naevius (ca. 270–ca. 201 B.C.).[5] The plays dealt with the exploits of famous Romans of history and legend, who wore the magisterial toga. This native invention competed with the Greek adaptations, but judging from ancient comments and the number of extant fragments of both forms, we must conclude that it was less popular.

Two types of comedy were developed. One was analogous to the *fabula praetexta.* Called the *fabula togata,* it was another native invention, a form of comedy played in Roman dress, hence the name "togaed." Only short fragments survive, so that we cannot construct plots, but from these remains and the titles of many plays we may postulate that they dealt with everyday characters interacting in ordinary situations. This tradition seems to have been on the whole more successful than the corresponding form on the tragic stage. It was not, however, nearly so popular as the other form of comedy, the *fabula palliata* or *comoedia palliata,* adapted from Greek plays and acted in Greek dress (the *pallium*).

The *Comoedia Palliata* Tradition.

Of the four dramatic forms popular in Rome during the second century B.C., complete plays survive only from the *comoedia palliata*—the twenty complete plays of Plautus and six of Terence. This tradition had a continuing influence on Roman letters and was known in revivals long after new works ceased to be written, sometime in the late second century B.C. In the fourth century of our era Aelius Donatus still found Terence of enough interest to write a commentary on his plays.

The *palliata* tradition was closely linked to the Greek theater, for the technique of its playwrights was to adapt plays from the Greek New Comedy for presentation on the Roman stage. Of the many fragments of New Comedy that have come down to us only a very few can be directly compared with the Latin comedies derived from them.[6] A great deal of scholarly effort has, however, been expended upon the method of adaptation.[7] This research has led to some interesting and curious attitudes toward Roman comedy.

Some extreme Hellenists have so grieved the loss of Greek New Comedy, and so elevated Greek literature at the expense of Latin, that they would treat Roman comedy as little more than a source of information about the fragmentary Greek tradition. These studies have often left the impression that the Romans were but translators, and not very accurate ones. Other scholars have worked carefully to establish the relationship between the plays of Plautus and Terence and their Greek models. Such studies have, in fact, done much to increase our understanding of the methods of the Roman playwrights, but they have also tended to divert attention from the study of Roman comedy as an independent dramatic tradition.

There is still much disagreement about the specifics of Roman adaptation; however, certain features can be delineated with confidence. First of all, we know of no sure example of a play in the *palliata* form that did not follow one or more Greek plays—it is usual to speak of a Greek "original," despite the negative connotations such a term may have for the intrinsic worth of the Roman play. It would be wrong to think of these plays, however, as translations in the modern sense. Greek comedy utilized verse forms developed for drama and others shared with lyric poetry. The Roman poets developed verse forms for their plays also, based on Greek patterns, but adapted to the Latin language. Not only does verse translation make close parallels between languages more difficult, but the Romans frequently wrote lyrical arias where the Greek New Comedy preferred less complicated meters, thus abandoning any attempt at verbal parallelism.

The freedoms taken with the plot and characters of a Greek play surely varied from playwright to playwright. We have some direct evidence as to how Plautus and Caecilius Statius handled passages of some length, which have survived in both their Greek and Latin versions, and there are statements in Donatus on modifications made by Terence on his originals. Some playwrights must have followed their texts rather closely; others— Plautus is a clear example—worked freely, changing monologue to dialogue, inserting long, metrically complex lyrics for singing, even bringing together material from different plays, a procedure to which Terence openly admits, citing Plautus, Naevius, and Ennius as precedents. We know from the prologues of Terence that practicing playwrights were much concerned about the treatment of their Greek material and may even have tried to formulate "gentlemen's agreements" in the hope of regularizing procedures.

Beyond the interests of literary history per se, at issue in this debate for the modern reader is the concept of originality. We tend to think first of freshness when speaking of the originality of an artist. Certainly, we expect a playwright to have the capacity to concoct his own plot and to invent his own characters. And yet, borrowing of theme, character, and even plot is a commonplace in Western literature. It is nowhere more prevalent than in the history of comedy. In fact, to a large extent it is custom that decides to which author an adaptation is ascribed. Molière's *Amphitryon* follows Plautus as closely as Plautus followed his models. Many modern translations of ancient comedy would have been known only by the names of their translators had they been produced in a different age. Originality, then, need not be judged by the pristine qualities of character and situation, but can be based on verve of expression, handling of theme, delineation of character. Certainly, the most successful of the *palliata* writers were original in these areas, or at least everything we know about their methods so suggests.

In fact, the history of the Roman stage indicates that for the Romans these adaptations were more attractive than the native drama with its novel plots. In tragedy, presentations based on Greek models were far more popular than the *fabula praetexta.* In comedy, *togata* plays held their own somewhat better against the *palliata* form, but they were still not as popular. It was, finally, the *comoedia palliata* that was revived in later periods and captured the attention of later critics and commentators. One might argue that more sophisticated Greek plays provided a pattern for the *palliata* poets superior to that of the clumsy native theater and so insured greater success, but, be that as it may, simple novelty was not a measure of success for the Romans.

Poets of the *Palliata* Tradition.   We have the names of many poets who wrote in the *comoedia palliata,* as well as many fragments to go with the complete plays of Plautus and Terence. These constitute a sufficient basis for some reasonable speculation about the tradition as a whole.[8] In addition, ancient sources make reference to poets of the *palliata* that can help in evaluating the principal figures.

Perhaps the most famous of these references is the so-called canon of Volcacius Sedigitus, a critic of the late second century before our era. It is in the form of a short poem quoted by Aulus Gellius (ca. A.D. 123–ca. 165) in his literary potpourri *The Attic Nights* (15.24). Volcacius sets out to inform the curious about the relative merits of the *palliata* poets. He lists ten of them, ordered thusly: Caecilius Statius, Plautus, Naevius, Licinius, Atilius, Terence, Turpilius, Trabea, Luscius Lanuvinus, Ennius. Of these little is known of Licinius, Atilius, Trabea, and Luscius Lanuvinus. The last, however, is known by reputation, for he was Terence's chief literary antagonist. Naevius and Turpilius have left more fragments than these, but it is hard to assess their work with accuracy. Ennius had great fame as the father of Roman epic, but little is known of him as a writer of comedy.

The list itself reflects the tastes of one critic, whose general competence or criteria for evaluation are unknown to us. That he ranked Caecilius Statius so high may seem surprising in view of the fact that only fragments of his work survive, but in antiquity his reputation was generally high.[9] Plautus has left us a considerable body of plays, a tribute, one might presume, to his popularity, so that we might expect him to be ranked near the top. That Terence is rated so far down the list also seems surprising, in view of the fact that his plays have survived whereas those of others have not. Possible explanations are that owing to his untimely death his volume of plays did not deserve comparison with more prolific writers, or that Volcacius reflects the prejudices of the establishment, which fought Terence in his lifetime and may have damned his memory,[10] or simply that Terence did not appeal to Volcacius's personal tastes. Under any circumstances, such a definitive list, coming from a source so near in age to the poets in question, has justly received notice, regardless of its limitations.

Another direct comparison of these poets was made by Marcus Terentius Varro (116–27 B.C.). Varro was the foremost scholar of his era, and a specialist in dramatic tradition. He records that in plot Caecilius Statius was best, in characterization Terence, and in dialogue Plautus.[11] This comment carries with it the respect accorded its author by modern scholarship, and can be made to square easily with the list of Volcacius, if we account for the relatively low position of Terence on nonliterary grounds.

The great teacher of rhetoric Quintilian (mid-first century of our era) also gave an evaluation of Roman comedy in his *Institutions* (10.1.99 ff.). He mentions Plautus, of whom, he records, Aelius Stilo (second and first centuries before our era) said that had the Muses wished to speak Latin they would have spoken in his style. We are told that the old critics praised Caecilius Statius (thus he confirms indirectly the evaluations of Volcacius and Varro). Quintilian, however, considers the works of Terence most elegant, although he repeats the old rumor that they may have been written by Scipio. Despite his remarks about the relative merits of the playwrights, however, Quintilian makes clear his view that the whole comic tradition was so inferior to Greek New Comedy as to make it Rome's weakest poetic genre.

Aulus Gellius denigrates the Roman stage in a similar manner.

He compares *The Necklace* of Caecilius Statius with the original play by Menander (*The Attic Nights,* 2.23), quoting parallel passages from each to support his observations, and concludes that the Roman poet is pleasant enough when read alone, but pales when compared to Menander.

Suetonius in his *Life of Terence* quotes short poems ascribed to Cicero and Julius Caesar that praise Terence. Both speak of his purity of language, for which he was famed throughout the classical period. Caesar calls him "half-Menander," meant, obviously, as a complimentary comparison. But he cites one significant shortcoming, the absence of *vis comica,* or "comic punch." It is generally assumed that Caesar was referring to the sparsity in Terence of broad, obvious humor, for on the whole his plays rely on careful characterization and manipulation of character interactions for their effects. He was not the first to make this observation. Terence had defended himself in his prologues against similar attacks by contemporary critics.

Terence's Place in the *Palliata* Tradition.   Plautus's comedy is well known to us. His plays are quite varied in theme, insofar as one may speak of variety within a tradition based so heavily on stock characters (the slave, the old man, the young lover, the grasping prostitute, etc.) and situations (husbands in search of relief from carping wives, young lovers frustrated by hardhearted mistresses and strict fathers, etc.).[12] Generally, however, they are robust and hearty, relying often on broad puns, vulgarities, and, surely, a great deal of visual humor arising from animated interchanges between the characters. He adapted plays from several Greek playwrights, including Menander, Terence's favorite source, but Menander was not his usual model. He was also a talented metrician who specialized in long lyrical passages, amounting to musical arias. Though the more intellectual effects of his plays may well be underestimated by the critical tradition, certainly the first impression of a typical Plautine play is that it offers much direct, often farcical good humor.

Plautus must have been an innovator in certain aspects of his work, for he stood quite near the beginning of the comic tradition in Rome. His style left a distinctive impression.[13] It has often been suggested that his younger contemporary, Caecilius Statius, who survived him by some sixteen years, was an important figure in changing the direction of his theater. Caecilius may have turned more toward Menander as a source and toned down the more outrageous behavior of Plautus's characters. He also exhibited less lyrical virtuosity. Certainly, Caecilius's considerable reputation suggests that his work was not routine, and whether or not he set out intentionally to write in a mode different from that of the tradition as he found it, his work was different in texture from that of Plautus.[14]

Terence, who lived at a time when the comic stage was a well-developed institution, may have been a quite independent figure. We cannot say that he was revolutionary, although the comedy of the only major figure after his death, Turpilius (d. 103 B.C.), does bear more resemblance to his work than to that of Plautus. Still, his style may have been only eccentric, rather than a major force in modifying the tradition. He was surely controversial during his lifetime, as the debates recorded in his prologues amply testify, and his problems with the poets' guild also suggest that he departed from traditional forms.[15] His plays are much quieter than those of Plautus, and much more obviously thoughtful. They do not have the lyrical flourish of the earlier poet, and they avoid his crudities, of both language and presentation. It is often suggested that they were aimed more at Terence's intellectual friends and patrons than at the unsophisticated Roman audience to whom Plautus presumably looked for his survival. His popular success did not come easy, but Caecilius, the acknowledged master of his day, if we may believe the prologue of Terence's *The Mother-in-Law,* had problems also in his early career. Terence himself achieved a measure of success in his own day by any standard. *The Eunuch* was remembered for its financial success. Even if we think Volcacius Sedigitus ranks Terence too low, we must remember that sixth is quite high enough among the total number of *palliata* playwrights to be worthy of recognition. By the time of Quintilian tastes seem to have been such that the great teacher of rhetoric ranks him at the head of what, however, he felt to be a mediocre lot.

For what significance it may have, we can observe that only Plautus and Terence survived the Middle Ages. The history of classical texts shows that some authors survive virtually by accident whereas superior contemporaries perish utterly, but there has generally been a correlation between survival and artistic ability. Whatever his place in the historical development of the *palliata* tradition, for Western letters Terence took his place next to Plautus and provided an important model for playwrights who sought a more sophisticated and urbane alternative to the older poet's frenetic vivacity.

Chapter Four

The Plays of Terence

General Considerations

Before one begins a study of Terence's plays, it will be useful to establish a context for what follows within the scholarly tradition. Much of the scholarship on any ancient author is manifestly technical, involving questions of grammar, metrics, textual criticism, and the like. This is especially true of the work on Roman comedy.

In addition to this type of study, there has been a history of research, which has dominated approaches to Roman comedy, into the relationship between Greek New Comedy and the Latin plays for which it provided dramatic models. Now, of the vast body of Greek comedy from which Roman playwrights drew material only some five plays survive more or less intact. All are by Menander, and none is the model for a surviving Roman play. Hence, the work of the scholar in this area is frequently a laborious and ingenious manipulation of fragmentary evidence in an effort to produce a patently speculative picture of a Greek comedy and the departures from it in a Latin survival.

The close historical connection between Greek and Roman comedy has also hampered the appreciation of the Roman stage as an independent phenomenon because of a tendency, arising in part from a fascination with the extinct, and in part from general philhellenism, to attempt to recapture in whatever fashion something of lost Greek literature.[1] Thus, Roman comedy per se is moved into the background, as Roman plays become documents that offer us broad hints about the nature of Greek plays. In this atmosphere, even when Roman comedy does become the focus of attention, it is treated often from a literary historical perspective. As valuable as such an approach can be for establishing an author's historical accomplishments, these studies frequently do not finally offer a treatment of Roman comedy in its own right.

It is with this background in mind, therefore, that the following discussion of the individual plays of Terence will be cast as much as possible in the direction of dealing with significant dramatic creations quite apart from their relationship with other literary issues. Certainly, we will refer to Terence's use of Greek material and consider his accomplishments in the light of his own times and of subsequent Western drama, but the primary goal will be to present the plays themselves, as the products of one of Western letters' most respected and influential playwrights.

The Girl from Andros (Andria)

Plot. The play revolves around the efforts of a young man to maintain his close, marriagelike relationship with a girl clearly unacceptable to his father. Its first scene, a conversation between Simo, the father, and Sosia, a freedman, establishes the background from which the plot develops: Pamphilus, a young man of about twenty, having shown himself of good character, agreeable disposition, and general reliability, has been betrothed by his father to the daughter of one Chremes, a neighbor and old friend. Quite recently, however, Simo has learned that his son is involved deeply with Glycerium, the sister of a foreign woman from the island of Andros, who had come to Athens some time before, had become a *hetaera* (a sort of prostitute with a limited, regular clientele), and had recently died. This involvement, now general knowledge, has led to the neighbor's withdrawal from the marriage agreement. Simo, fearing the Andrian girl may bring his son real problems, is planning to force the young man into abandoning the affair and taking a respectable wife. In order to further this project, he proposes to pretend the wedding is still to take place, despite Chremes' withdrawal, so that his son will defy his legitimate, patriarchal demand that he marry. Such defiance would provide a reason for him to use his authority fully and demand that his son break off the affair. Without such an excuse, however, he feels that his demand might be viewed as an arbitrary interference.

This opening scene is followed immediately by an encounter between Simo and Davus, a family slave who serves as Pamphilus's valet. Simo confronts Davus and warns him to do nothing to upset the wedding plans, as he has learned to expect the slave to maneuver on the young man's behalf. On Simo's departure, Davus, in monologue, reveals his own deep concern about the situation. Glycerium is pregnant; the lovers are resolved to acknowledge the child; they are fomenting wild rumors such as that Glycerium is in reality an Athenian citizen.

The play now begins to progress more quickly. Glycerium is actually in labor. Pamphilus himself meets the household maid as she is going for a midwife. He promises to stand by Glycerium despite his father's wedding arrangements. Enter Charinus, a friend of Pamphilus, distraught at learning of Pamphilus's betrothal, since he himself had hoped to sue for Philumena, Chremes' daughter. The two thus discover their mutual repugnance for Pamphilus's impending marriage, and are opportunely met by Davus, who, in the course of searching for Pamphilus, has been near Chremes' house and has concluded from the lack of unusual activity that the wedding plans must be a ruse. He reasons that Simo's deception may provide Pamphilus with just the opportunity he needs to put off his father: he must feign a willingness to submit to Simo's demands in order to frustrate his father's immediate plans in the hope that something will happen to improve the situation before Simo can find another means of pressing him.

Simo arrives on cue, and Pamphilus tells him he is prepared to do his filial duty by marrying the girl of his father's choice. Instead of frustrating Simo, however, the news rekindles his hopes. He begs Chremes, who enters on the heels of Pamphilus's exit, intent on clearing up a rumor that Simo is continuing the wedding plans even after his withdrawal, to reconsider and finally convinces him to pledge his daughter once again.

The young men are suitably (and comically) perturbed at discovering themselves undone by Davus's cleverness. Davus continues to work desperately, while Pamphilus resolves to admit everything if worse comes to worst. The slave hopes to alienate Chremes again by convincing him of the truth: that Glycerium's child is by Pamphilus. Proving the obvious requires deception, however, since Chremes has been warned about Davus's tricks, so Davus and Glycerium's maid go through a comic charade for the old man's benefit. The importance of the scheme is undercut, however, by the arrival of Crito, a relative of the deceased sister.

Crito resolves the situation, for he reports that Glycerium

is in fact the orphaned daughter of an Athenian citizen, thus an appropriate marriage partner for Pamphilus. Simo, already beside himself that his plans for Pamphilus's marriage have been destroyed, is forced to listen to this account, only because Chremes is acquainted with Crito and so vouches for his honesty. Moreover, in the course of telling Glycerium's story, Crito relates details which reveal Glycerium to be none other than Chremes' long-lost daughter. Thus, the path is clear for the lovers to marry, and, incidentally, for Charinus to sue for the hand of Chremes' remaining daughter.[2]

A word about the nature of this plot with respect to the traditions of New Comedy and to Terence's other works will perhaps be useful. Terence utilizes the traditions of his stage completely. This is not to imply that he lacks creativity, for the discussion of structure that follows will aptly demonstrate that such is not the case. On the other hand, Terence's audience was thoroughly familiar not only with the character types in the play, but with the incidents themselves. The old father often stands in the way of his young son's love interests. The family slave often leads the effort to neutralize the father and accommodate the son. Furthermore, the audience knows that boy will finally get girl. When Davus mentions, for example, the rumor that Glycerium is really an Athenian, the audience suspects that she will be found to be just that. The fortuitous sequence of events that brings everything together is also traditional. As contrived as the ending seems, the audience would not be offended, for they were long schooled on such dramatic ploys. But, as formulaic as were the individual parts, the whole that they made was always different, so that the audience could indulge in the pleasure not so much of surprise as of anticipation of "how it will go this time."

Structure.   *The Girl from Andros* offers an excellent opportunity for studying Terence's dramatic structures. It is by tradition the first of his plays, although we have seen elsewhere (chap. 1) how uncertain the evidence for Terentian chronologies can be. In fact, the play's structure has often been cited as internal evidence for its early date. It is not constructed along the lines Terence favored strongly in most of his work, but the construction, it can be cogently argued, does exhibit features that are more or less embryonic of the "preferred" form exhibited by four of his six plays.

Another interesting feature of *The Girl from Andros* is that we have quite good evidence for Terence's strategy in forming his plot. The play's prologue indicates clearly that he took material from two plays by Menander, *The Girl from Andros,* the main source, and *The Girl from Perinthos,* a play with a very similar plot. We learn from the commentator Donatus, who had both Greek plays available for comparison with Terence's work, that Terence had invented the characters of the young man Charinus and slave Byrria rather than taking them from his models.[3] Again, we shall see that this is a perceptible step in the direction of Terence's other plots.

The introduction of Charinus means that *The Girl from Andros* has two young men. It also has two old men, and the suggestion of two plot lines: the resolution of Pamphilus's problems and the securing of a girl for Charinus. We find, therefore, a rudimentary form of a method of composition commonly called the "duality method."

The Girl from Andros does not show this structure in its most developed form. The similarities and contrasts between the pairs of characters might have been more sharply drawn, and a second intrigue centering on Charinus's frustrated suit is never really developed into a bona fide subplot. What we have, however, is the opportunity to see the "duality method" in skeletal form.[4]

A second feature of the play's structure is the absence of an expository prologue. Although it was not unprecedented for an ancient comedy to omit the prologue, we usually find an introductory speech providing information about the upcoming action, frequently even a plot summary.[5] Terence eschewed the prologue as a device for setting his scene, but retained the form as a means through which he debated with his literary enemies. He goes to the trouble at times of alerting the audience not to expect plot exposition (cf. *Ad.* 22–24), making it clear that his practice was unusual. Without an informative prologue, then, Terence's opening scenes bore more of a burden for adumbrating dramatic development than those of other plays in the tradition that he inherited.

In the first scene of *The Girl from Andros,* the conversation

between Simo and his freedman Sosia offers a good example
of his technique. Donatus remarked specially on the inventive
qualities of this scene and singled out Terence's modifications
of the forms of his two Menandrian models, changes made to
further his own dramatic purposes. The results have not always
been so admired by critics,[6] but an examination of the scene
will show that it works well at several levels and generally justifies Donatus's enthusiasm for it.

The first purpose is to establish the situation. This is accomplished through a conversation in which Simo tells the freedman
Sosia about his plan to trick his son into believing that he is
to marry a girl picked by his father. The fact that the freedman
is somewhat outside the situation allows Simo to recount past
conditions and present circumstances without appearing silly,
whereas Menander had begun one play with a monologue, the
other with a conversation between the old man and his wife.
Thus, he establishes for us his son's generally commendable
past conduct, leading to his betrothal to Chremes' daughter;
the unfortunate involvement with the Andrian woman's sister,
leading to Chremes' withdrawal; his fears for Pamphilus's future;
his concern that the slave Davus will interfere with his plans.

We are, in fact, presented with a situation familiar in New
Comedy. The audience, out of its experience with the stock
forms of New Comedy, knows that the plot will revolve around
the efforts to help two young lovers, and even that the young
girl will eventually be discovered to be an acceptable marriage
partner so that the two may be united. The comic action of
the play will be centered on the thwarting of the father, and
schemes to that end will probably be devised by the slave. Terence knew his audience's conditioning, and so could develop
his background with economy. It was the particular working
out of this situation, not its uniqueness, which would excite
the spectator.

The art of the scene, however, lies in Terence's ability to
handle this necessary plot exposition in a way which enables
him at the same time to develop his characters and to anticipate
his theme. Some have objected that despite the changes from
Menander, for Simo to recite information about his son to a
close family retainer is unrealistic to the point of clumsiness.
In fact, the freedman's familiarity with Pamphilus has its advan-

tages. He is not so involved on a day-to-day basis that it is totally ridiculous for Simo to be talking to him in this way, especially given the human need to discuss matters with old friends even to the point of dwelling on the obvious. On the other hand, his reactions to Simo's statements about Pamphilus's character offer good confirmation of their accuracy.[7] Thus, the interchange gives us a good baseline against which we may evaluate Pamphilus when he appears.

At the same time, we are learning about Simo from the way in which he presents his case to Sosia. Now, one theme of *The Girl from Andros,* stated very succinctly, is the relationship of father and son. In this scene we are, quite appropriately, learning about the son from the father, and about the father from the way he talks about the son. By choosing Sosia as a third party to interact with Simo, Terence promotes these effects. We may conclude from his choice to modify his models that he clearly intended to do so.

We may turn to the character pairs, which are an important feature of the play's structure. As we have seen, pairs of characters are an integral part of "duality" composition. In this play the pairs are the two old men, Simo and Chremes, the two youths, Pamphilus and Charinus, and the two slaves, Davus and Byrria.

Of these pairs the Simo-Chremes relationship is the better developed. It is important to developing the theme of the play that Simo be driven to greater and greater extremes by his concerns and frustrations. We see him best when compared with Chremes. He can beg Chremes earnestly to risk his daughter's happiness in an attempt to divert Pamphilus from his folly. In contrast, Chremes consistently tries to reconcile in reasonable fashion his concern as a parent with his duty as a friend. We find the climax of this tension near the end of the play in Chremes' rebuke of Simo for his unreasonable requests:

You compelled me to offer my daughter to a young man much involved in another love affair, shrinking away from anything to do with a wife, to subject her to upheavals and an uncertain marriage so that I could cure your son at the expense of her toil and grief. You implored. I started into it, while the situation allowed. Now the situation's different. Face it. (827–32)

Terence utilizes Chremes as more than a simple character foil, however. While we are primarily interested in Simo for his relationship with Pamphilus, Chremes is used more freely within the plot. He becomes the target of Davus's most elaborate scheme when he and the maid, Mysis, convince him that Pamphilus is the father of Glycerium's child (740 ff.). He must vouch for the stranger, Crito, and so hold Simo at bay while the story of Glycerium's birth is unfolded. Finally, he is, of course, discovered to be Glycerium's father, so that the play can be neatly finished with Pamphilus ready to marry Chremes' daughter after all.

The Pamphilus-Charinus pair is used with somewhat less richness. Yet, we will recall that Terence took pains to write Charinus into his play, and so may conclude that he was interested in having a "pair" of young men. The effect is that Charinus's immature complaining becomes a good point of comparison by which the relative strength of Pamphilus's character is made clear. Also, Charinus's presence is enough to suggest a more complicated plot, which must also accommodate his desire to marry Philumena. Although the second plot is not developed, the suggestion of it was enough to inspire the so-called second ending, the chief function of which is a clearer resolution of Charinus's situation.

Finally, Davus and Byrria are paired. One need not make too much of this, but these characters clearly work together, as do the other pairs. Davus, the active schemer, is contrasted with the passive tattletale and bearer of bad news, Byrria, who can provide no positive program to address the young men's problems. The comparison is slight, but perceptible, and it is indicative of the plan by which Terence structured his play.

Characters.   Terence has been praised since antiquity for the quality of his characterizations.[8] Perhaps *The Girl from Andros* does not show his talent at its best,[9] but it does illustrate well his ability to develop within the stock types with which dramatic tradition peopled its stages distinctive features that are pivotal for relaying the messages of his plays. Each of the five principal figures deserves our attention: Simo, Chremes, Pamphilus, Charinus, and Davus. We should also consider the more important features of the minor characters.

Simo. In our discussion of structure we have seen how the two old men, Simo and Chremes, are contrasted in such a way as to focus upon Simo's character. Since the relationship between Simo and his son, Pamphilus, is a key element in the play's theme, the gradual revelation of Simo's shortcomings is a major concern. Before the action is over we will find Simo, the father, ineffective in fulfilling his parental role because he lacks a true understanding of his son's character. Pamphilus, on the other hand, will grow in stature until he has assumed the responsibilities of a Roman father.[10] Thus, we must look at the richness Terence gives to Simo's role in order to avoid the mistake of categorizing him merely as the stock comic father who must be circumvented in order for his son to get his girl.

The initial scene of the play, important as it is for presenting the background to the audience, is, as we have seen, constructed also with a view toward forming for us our "baseline" impressions of both Simo and his son. The son's character is established by what is said about him by his father and the freedman. The father is portrayed by what he himself says.

Simo's account of his dealings with Pamphilus reveals the cautious attention he had paid his son. He was pleased to see him developing into a personality congenial to his own rather conservative views. His style had been to avoid direct interference in his son's affairs, especially since Pamphilus appeared to be progressing so nicely. Beneath his account, however, we can see Simo's own system of values: he found Pamphilus successful because he found favor with others. Simo approves of the middle road, of a son liked by everyone because his neutral opinions offend no one (cf. 62–66). He is shocked by Pamphilus's love affair largely because it marks such an unexpected break with form. The compliant, moderate young man is suddenly fervent in his affair with Glycerium and willing to maintain it despite all good appearances. In fact, although Simo has been genuinely concerned for his son's success and well-being and has carefully monitored his development, he has not acquired firsthand knowledge of the boy's character. His motives have been admirable, but his instincts were flawed. Thus, he did not have the confidence to approach his son directly, and as the play progresses he becomes so frustrated in his efforts to deal with the situation through indirect methods that he loses all sense of balance. The prospect of Pamphilus's ruination drives him to beg Chremes to risk his daughter's happiness in order to encumber Pamphilus with a safe marriage. He defines that ruin in thoroughly traditional terms, however, as the loss of good repute, without a real knowledge of the solidity of Pamphilus's character.

In the end Simo shows the danger of a too inflexible approach to the problems of fatherhood. His commendable interest in his son's well-being is not enough in itself, for he is too concerned about the outward reflections of Pamphilus's behavior to be able to understand his son's own motives for his actions. He is not sufficiently analytical or trusting in his son's finer qualities to carry him beyond his need to evaluate success and failure almost totally in terms of outward appearances. He is a sympathetic figure: a decent man whose shortcomings are unfortunately such that they prevent him from exercising his fatherly functions effectively.

Chremes.   As we have seen in our section on structure, Chremes' most important function is as a foil for Simo. Thus, Terence did not need to individualize his character to any great extent. His most important trait is his consistently reasonable approach to problems. He, too, is a father, and his concern for his daughter's welfare is not less great than that of Simo for his son. He had sought Pamphilus for a son-in-law when he believed he had seen enough of the young man's good conduct. When, on the strength of considerable evidence, he finds that Pamphilus is unsuitable after all, he moves to protect his daughter from harm. Presented with Simo's pleas, and his assurances that the situation with Pamphilus has changed, he cautiously agrees to reconsider. When he learns that Simo's expectations for Pamphilus's estrangement from Glycerium have not been realized, he moves once more to protect his daughter. In each of these actions he reacts appropriately to the evidence.

From another point of view Chremes contrasts with Simo as a father. He fulfills that role much more effectively than does Simo because he does, in fact, achieve what is best for Philumena through his straightforward approach.

Although Chremes is not a particularly rich character, his is an important part, and it achieves its dramatic peak in the scene with Davus and Mysis. The scene is crucial to the play's pacing, for without it the last third of the play would be overly static. Chremes' "straight" reactions to Davus and the maid, who is bewildered by the slave's tricks and always on the verge of ruining things, must be timed well so that Davus's antics will be allowed their full comic effect. Stock character though Chremes is, Terence makes full use of him.

Pamphilus. Pamphilus is the most significant character in *The Girl from Andros.* He evolves in rather the opposite direction from Simo: whereas the father is a good person, whose defects come to light under the pressures of the situation, the son grows and matures into his potential.

As we have seen, Terence takes pains to establish the character of his young protagonist before his arrival on stage through Simo's conversation with Sosia.[11] The puzzle is how we are to understand his lapse from responsible conduct into a too close involvement with the young foreigner. Not only is his father unnerved by the prospect, but his personal slave Davus is also concerned that his young master has gone too far (206 ff.). Terence's comic stage admitted several types of young men, and so, although his audience might expect that the love affair would end happily, they could not predict exactly what Pamphilus's character would be or to what extent it would have bearing on the play's outcome.

When Pamphilus makes his appearance, we are eager to see him for ourselves. The situation is such that he reveals himself quickly. He enters complaining about his father's actions: "Is it decent to do this, to undertake it? Is this acting like a father?" (236). Things become worse when he learns of Glycerium's condition from the maid Mysis as she is going for a midwife. Mysis is concerned that he will abandon them under pressure from his father. Pamphilus eagerly reaffirms his love and support and makes it quite clear that he considers Glycerium his complete responsibility.[12] The earnestness of his emotion is neither immature nor foolish. The claim has been made that this is the first example in Western letters of honorable love between unmarried persons.[13] What is lacking, however, is any sense of how he can fulfill his promises. Much of Pamphilus's maturation comes from his developing the character to face these difficulties squarely.

This meeting with Mysis is followed directly by an exchange

with Charinus (301 ff.). Charinus acts, of course, as a foil character to Pamphilus. Their conversation underscores the relative
maturity of Pamphilus as compared with his young contemporary. Despite the rashness of his claims to Mysis, Pamphilus
can still advise action rather than whining: "If you or Byrria
[Charinus's slave] can do anything, do it, invent it, find it, get
her [Philumena] given to you. I'll work on her not being given
to me" (333–34). This exchange is typical of their respective
roles, for in general Charinus will play the passive complainer
to Pamphilus's man of action.

Even more significant than this relationship, however, is that
of Pamphilus and Davus. Slaves are the most visible of all New
Comedy's stock characters.[14] There are a number of types, but
often a slave takes the protagonist's role as the motivator of
most of the comic action. Frequently the slave is much more
the true master than the passive young owner, who relies on
him for the intelligence and courage to solve his problems.
Therefore, when Davus enters (line 338), self-important in his
conviction that he has discovered Simo's ruse and so can give
Pamphilus advice on how to check the plan, we expect that
Pamphilus will put himself in his slave's hands. And so he does,
initially, although from the beginning Pamphilus only reluc-
tantly follows the plan of pretending to submit to his father's
demands that he marry.

This ploy leads to the total collapse of Pamphilus's situation,
to a renewal of Mysis's fears that Glycerium is to be abandoned,
and to Charinus's charges of duplicity. Pamphilus reacts to all
this, however, in a much more positive way than young lovers
of the usual sort. He can say, "I admit that I've gotten what
was coming to me, since I'm so lazy and witless as to have
put my fortunes in the hands of this worthless slave! I'm paying
the price for my stupidity . . ." (607–10). He can reassure
Charinus by saying, "If we can work it so that my father doesn't
know that I'm the cause for the marriage's not taking place,
good. But if we can't, I'll do the simple thing, let him know
I'm the cause" (699–701). Finally, by the time of his confrontation with Simo, Pamphilus has gained enough presence and
courage to say, "I confess that I love her. If that's wrong, I
confess this too. I put myself under your control, father: put
on me whatever burden you wish; give your orders. You want

me to marry? To give her up? I'll bear it the best I can" (896–98).

In summary, the young man will finally not fit the mold of the fatuous young lover. He has shown a genuine willingness to accept the burden of his situation and has struggled manfully to resolve the crisis arising out of the conflict between loyalty to his mistress, for whom he has assumed all moral responsibility, and duty to his father. He does not achieve perfect balance in his attempts at solution, but he shows commendable spirit and genuine moral worth. His growth of character is one of the play's most attractive features.

Charinus. We have seen that the character of Charinus serves an important structural purpose as a contrast to Pamphilus. In his own right, however, he represents a standard character type. He is the young man who cannot find a way to attain his beloved through his own designs and must turn to others as a sort of helpless supplicant. Such young men rely first on their slaves, then on their friends.

In this instance, Byrria, Charinus's slave, is a rather ineffective figure who never really helps his master at all. In fact, he disturbs his life more than anything else with his reports on the status of Pamphilus's wedding. Charinus, therefore, puts himself in the hands of Davus and Pamphilus. Under any circumstances, it is just this submissiveness that makes Charinus such a good foil for Pamphilus. The individuality with which Terence has imbued Pamphilus is all the more clear when contrasted with the quite orthodox treatment of his friend Charinus.

The atmosphere created by this stock figure can be seen from the so-called second ending of *The Girl from Andros.* This material, which was added probably during the Roman imperial period (ca. A.D. 100?), makes specific the granting of Charinus's wish to marry Philumena. This issue had been dealt with in the original version only by Pamphilus's comment that they should go inside to arrange a bethrothal with Chremes (line 980). The second ending is clearly in reaction to an audience expectation. Young men of Charinus's type always fare well enough in the end, when someone else arranges for their marriages or access to their favorite lovers.

Davus. The character of the family slave is perhaps the most memorable one in Roman comedy. Davus is a generally unremarkable member of that clan. He is neither passive (like his counterpart, Byrria), nor a dominating force who carries the action. We find in him just enough of the fascinating schemer to know his type. Simo's concern that he will try to interfere with his plans and his confrontation with Davus on this account (173 ff.) make clear that he is to occupy this role.

Davus vacillates, in fact, between the gleeful trickster and a figure genuinely sensitive to the problems Pamphilus has created for himself. His soliloquy following Simo's warnings shows us this side of him. Despite his fear that if caught violating Simo's direct interdict "[Simo] will send me headlong to the grist mill," (214) he still declares:

I've got another problem on top of this: whether this Andrian girl is his wife or his mistress, she's pregnant by Pamphilus. It's worth the effort to listen to their audacity—an undertaking of lunatics not lovers. They've decided to claim whatever child is born. . . . (215–19)

This speech shows the slave's genuine concern for his young master. This sensitivity goes far toward confirming a general seriousness of purpose in the relationship between Pamphilus and Glycerium. Despite the vainness of their hopes, Davus treats them with a certain tenderness.

On the other hand, Davus exhibits obvious delight at discovering the old man's ruse and at the prospect of using it against him (337 ff.). When one scheme misfires, he moves to another. We see him in his final glory when he conspires with the maid Mysis to convince Chremes that the child just born is indeed Pamphilus's (740 ff.).

In the end, though, as we have seen already, Pamphilus rises to face his own problems, and the solution to the play's dilemma comes from circumstances outside Davus's contrivances. Some have seen this very fact as a weakness.[15] It is, however, well in keeping with the role Terence has set for Davus, and the characterization he intends for Pamphilus, that the tricks of the slave not be the means for duping Simo. That set of characters is for another sort of play.

Byrria, Crito, Mysis. The minor characters of *The Girl from Andros* require no extended analysis. Byrria is a cipher, used primarily as a means of carrying rumors to his master. His appearance has some importance in the play's structure, but his character is slight. Crito's part is a good one in that he occupies the stage prominently during the denouement (904 ff.). It is important that he strike the proper chord of honesty to insure credibility for his report, but he has nothing special to offer by way of characterization.

Mysis is a more interesting figure. She has a small part that affects the plot in an important way. Terence uses her interchange with Pamphilus to develop the young man's character, and she has a major comic scene with Davus when they conspire against Chremes. She is basically the stock character of an older maid, but she has the opportunity for these two good scenes, and her commitment to her young mistress adds some dimension to her.

Theme. Ancient authorities long ago labeled the products of New Comic writers as *motoria* (active), *stataria* (quiet), and mixed, based on the physical effort required to act them. Of Terence's work *Phormio* and *The Eunuch* are "active," *The Girl from Andros* and *The Brothers* "mixed," *The Self-Tormentor* and *The Mother-in-Law* "quiet." Compared with Plautus's most lively pieces, however, all of Terence seems rather "quiet." Terence based none of his plays on the melding of many scenes aimed at eliciting raucous laughter (his lack of *vis comica* noted by Caesar?). The interactions of his characters and his fine touch with language have been the features upon which his reputation through the ages has rested.

In comedies dominated by scenes of broad, often farcical laughter our impression of theme tends to be formed principally on the basis of plot content. We are, for example, more taken with the incidents of Aristophanes' *Birds* than with the interaction of his characters in a more personal sense. We rarely think explicitly about the theme of a Marx Brothers presentation while we watch, even though there are often satirical themes at issue. With Terence the theme, which emerges from character interaction even more than from plot, is an important, overt factor in our appreciation of the play.

The Girl from Andros is a typical case in point. Like many of the plays of New Comedy, its theme can be stated succinctly and is not earth-moving in its implications. But these themes touch everyone just because they are so close to those of daily life ("Oh life, oh Menander, which copied the other?") For this play we can state the issue simply: *The Girl from Andros* deals, broadly, with love.

To explicate this bald statement a bit, we can observe two types of relationships, that of parent and child and that of friends and lovers. Terence presents us quite a complex of specific relationships: Simo-Pamphilus, Chremes-Philumena, Simo-Chremes, Davus-Pamphilus, Mysis-Glycerium, Pamphilus-Charinus, and, of course, Pamphilus-Glycerium. In addition to this basic theme, there is an important related issue: communication and true understanding between father and son.

We have seen elsewhere the comparison between Simo and Chremes as fathers. The concept of fatherhood is, in fact, central to the theme of the play. Simo presents us with an interesting study of how a well-meaning father can suffer a significant failure in his relationship with his son.

Chremes deals with his daughter's situation in a quite direct manner. It is the responsibility of the Roman father to arrange marriages for his daughters. Although premarital courtship and agreement between young people beforehand might not have been a major feature of the process, the loving father would, of course, assess the prospects of his daughter's genuine happiness. This is just what we find Chremes doing. Pamphilus's conduct and good reputation suggested him as a fine candidate for his daughter's husband. When his conduct took an unexpected turn, Chremes withdrew his proposal for the sake of his daughter's security. He consistently reacts to the situation on this basis, and we can only approve of his actions. In fact, our only cause for disapproval might be his decision to reinstate his offer of marriage when Simo insists that Pamphilus's circumstances have changed. He argues that it will be a good risk for Chremes because of the opportunity to resurrect a good young man and so acquire a fine son-in-law (565 ff.). We might feel that any risk is too great where his daughter's happiness is concerned, but Chremes is a concerned friend as well as a good father.

In the case of Simo, we have seen how his character exhibits some defects which adversely affect his relationship with his son. He has watched Pamphilus without interacting with him. He has intentionally not interfered with his son's exercising the privileges of young adulthood, but that noninterference has resulted in Simo's being unprepared to understand or cope directly with Pamphilus's unexpected behavior. He does not know his son's fundamental character well enough to assess the depth and purity of his devotion to Glycerium. Nor does he have the avenues of communication established to confront his son directly. Clearly, the situation between Simo and Pamphilus is touching and affects us with some seriousness, despite the fact that it is set among the stock relationships of New Comedy.

Terry McGarrity has argued in an interesting essay that *The Girl from Andros* presents us, in fact, with a sort of inversion of roles, in which the true father, Simo, falls short of his potential, whereas the son, Pamphilus, achieves success in terms traditionally paternal, both literally, in the birth of a child, and figuratively, in his relationship with Glycerium and his accepting of responsibility. This is a useful perspective. The relationship between the lovers is a much more satisfactory pact in human terms than that between Simo and Pamphilus. There is understanding, protection, and reciprocated affection between the two lovers. Against this background Pamphilus's character grows during the course of the play, as we find him acquiring a father's sense of responsibility.[16]

In another area, it is Pamphilus who intuits the ultimate value of direct communication. Although he would prefer his problems to be resolved without the trauma of direct confrontation, he assures Charinus that if there is no solution at hand, he will talk to his father directly (699–701). At the end of the play he does talk with Simo, giving final affirmation of his love and dutifulness by saying that he will try to give Glycerium up if his father remains unbending (896–98).

Through this complex of relationships Terence explores a simple theme. Fathers and sons often do become crossed in their purposes. Simo might have trusted enough in Pamphilus's fundamental worth to confront him directly with his concerns. Pamphilus might have gone directly to his father had the lines of communication been better established. And yet, *The Girl from Andros* is a very positive play, not just because of its rather contrived happy ending. Throughout it demonstrates and affirms the positive value of supportive relationships. Mysis will stand by Glycerium; Pamphilus is sympathetic to his friend Charinus and considers his happiness along with his own; Davus has a genuine affection for his young master; Chremes is more than patient with his friend Simo.

If it is useful to talk sometimes of the reintegration of a "blocking figure" into society, as Frye has done,[17] we may look for that phenomenon in the case of Simo. He truly loves his son, but he is the chief stumbling block to his happiness. The irony is all the greater that he has mishandled the present situation in the light of the very positive relationships which are so prominent in the play. The successful development of Pamphilus's paternal skills makes the irony all the more severe. But, in the end, the happy conclusion, contrived with typical New Comic efficiency, is complete not because Pamphilus and Glycerium (as well as Charinus and Philumena) are united, but because Simo and Pamphilus will be united. Both have had the opportunity to benefit from their experiences.

The Self-Tormentor (Heautontimorumenos)

Plot. Chremes, a farmer in the region outside Athens, confronts his neighbor, Menedemus, who, having bought his own farm recently, joins his slaves daily in hard labor. Chremes forces him to explain his behavior: his only son, Clinia, had become involved with a poor, foreign girl who came to Athens with an old woman from Corinth, treating her virtually as his wife; he had criticized his son so much that the young man left Athens to become a mercenary in an eastern army. Remorseful at having driven his son away, Menedemus resolved to punish himself until his son's return.

After this introductory scene the action quickens. Clitipho reports to his father, Chremes, that Clinia has returned and is at their house, but that his arrival should be kept from Menedemus. After his father leaves, we learn that he too has a mistress unbeknownst to his father, but whereas Clinia's Antiphila is a modest, devoted girl, his Bacchis is a typical courtesan with extravagant tastes.

Clinia enters to discuss with Clitipho his concern that Antiphila has been corrupted by other admirers in his absence. They are met by Syrus, Clitipho's slave, who had been sent to bring Antiphila to Clinia. He assures Clinia of Antiphila's continued devotion, and reports that he has also brought Bacchis with a retinue of attendants. She had been demanding a thousand drachmas promised her by Clitipho. Clitipho is afraid of his father's learning about his affair, but Syrus plans to pass her off as Clinia's mistress and pretend that Antiphila is her servant. Thereby Antiphila can be near Clinia, and Bacchis can be kept busy until they can find the money.

The action is continued the next morning. Chremes, despite Clinia's wishes, tells Menedemus of his son's return. He warns Menedemus, however, about Bacchis's rapacity, when Menedemus shows an inclination to give his son anything. At last he convinces him that any money should appear to have been bilked from him by Syrus, for to give openly might encourage even more excess.

To this purpose Chremes exhorts Syrus to find a way of getting Clinia money from Menedemus. The slave, amazed at his luck in finding Chremes eager to abet a scheme to raise money, agrees to take up the challenge. He relates a sketchy plan to convince Menedemus that Antiphila has come to Bacchis as surety on a thousand-drachma loan to a Corinthian woman who is now dead, but who had brought her from Caria; perhaps the old man can be induced to redeem her with the prospect of ransoming her home at a profit.

The situation changes suddenly, however, when Sostrata, Chremes' wife, comes out of their house to deliver astounding news. Some years before she had been ordered by Chremes to destroy their newborn daughter. Instead of doing this herself, she gave the task to a Corinthian woman, putting a ring as a token of patrimony with the baby. The ring has just been discovered in Antiphila's possession. Chremes is now well disposed toward having a daughter, and they go inside to find out whether Antiphila is indeed their child. Syrus must find a new scheme.

Clinia enters, delighted at the turn of events, and Syrus confronts him with his new plan. He asks that Clinia take Bacchis to his father's house, expose her as Clitipho's mistress, and ask that a marriage with Antiphila be arranged. Although Chremes is not likely to pledge his daughter, for he is expecting some scheme such as asking money for a pretended wedding, the situation may become confused enough to give more time to look for Clitipho's money.

The transfer is made; Syrus tells Chremes the truth about the relationships between the women and young men. The old man reacts as predicted, refusing to pledge his daughter to Clinia, but Syrus reminds him of the debt for which Antiphila is surety. Chremes gives him a thousand drachmas for Bacchis so that there will be no question of Antiphila's status.

Menedemus enters to tell Chremes of his new information and to ask for Antiphila's hand on Clinia's behalf. His hopes for Clinia's reconstruction are dashed by Chremes' self-satisfied assurances that the whole story is part of the scheme. He exits, despondent, but soon returns in vindication, able to relate to Chremes a story of intimacy between Clitipho and Bacchis that confirms his earlier report. Chremes is now crushed and in order to chasten his son agrees to the marriage of Antiphila and Clinia, stipulating that he will disinherit Clitipho in favor of Clinia.

Clitipho is beside himself at the news. Syrus suggests that, from the way he is being treated, one might think he is not Chremes and Sostrata's true son. The young man rushes off to confront his mother with this new fear. Sostrata, touched by her son's hurt, implores Chremes to relent. Chremes assures Clitipho of his legitimacy, and, urged also by Menedemus, reconsiders his decision, but on condition that Clitipho properly marry. Clitipho agrees, and all ends happily, even with assurances that Syrus will be pardoned.

The plot of *The Self-Tormentor* calls for some brief comment. It is certainly not among the simpler story lines of Roman comedy. It requires that the audience follow several changes of plan by Syrus: Bacchis is at first passed off as Clinia's mistress and Antiphila as her maid; then Syrus talks with Chremes about a plan to trick Menedemus; next Sostrata reports finding the ring in Antiphila's possession. Syrus concocts another plan, which never materializes, but he gets the money from Chremes by no more complicated means than telling him that Antiphila is surety on a forfeited debt; Bacchis is moved to Menedemus's house and finally recognized as Clitipho's mistress; Clinia and Antiphila are betrothed; Clitipho is disinherited; Chremes finally relents. Furthermore, the solution to Clinia's dilemma does not come from Syrus's machinations at all, but from the fortuitous recognition of Antiphila's true identity. All this is not prepared in advance, and the connection between Antiphila's recognition and the eventual solution to the plot must be grasped only after the fact. The twists are so unpredictable that some scholars think the difficulties are in fact created by Terence in modifying a more straightforward plot of Menander and omitting a prologue that explained the plot in some detail.

Terence knew, of course, that he was relying more on characterization than plot to achieve his effect. The evidence suggests that it was a successful play; those who think that Roman audiences could react only to simple plots must recall this piece as an example of a rather complicated plot line that seemed to receive a positive hearing.[18]

Structure. In his prologue Terence informs his audience that his play is a "single comedy from a single Greek play" and that the new offering "has been made double-plot from a simple plot (4–6)." As we have seen elsewhere, the playwrights of Terence's time argued over techniques of adapting Greek plays; Terence is serving notice that his play is from a single Greek original not heretofore seen on the Roman stage, but that he has modified its plot.

Predictably, such an assertion has intrigued modern scholars. It offers the prospect of glimpsing something of a lost play of Menander and of understanding better Terence's methods of adaptation. Scholars point to infelicities in the structure of the play that might be explained in terms of Terence's modifications. Some of the points raised in these discussions help to focus on the structure of *The Self-Tormentor*.[19] For example, the cryptic remark that a single plot was doubled would seem to underscore Terence's interest in "duality" construction.[20] *The Self-Tormentor* exhibits all the elements of that form: two love affairs produce complications that intertwine toward a conclusion and several pairs of characters are used to develop one another.

We will examine the question of duality a bit later. Let us look first at some of the problems in the play's structure.

Problems of Dramatic Structure. Three difficulties are of interest to us here. One arises from the somewhat precipitous entrances and exits, especially of Chremes. Another results from the incompleteness of Syrus's plans, which seem to lack clarity and leave us a bit confused. Finally, a third comes from the general complication of the plot, which may be criticized for using the discovery of Antiphila's identity rather inorganically, for changing directions too quickly, and for confusing us unnecessarily with Syrus's malformed schemes.

Examples of Chremes' rapid exits and entrances are found at lines 170 and 502. At line 170 he has just finished his initial conversation with Menedemus and turns his attention to the dinner party he has planned for the evening. He wants to tell his neighbor Phania that it is time to come to dinner, saying at line 170, "I'll go see if he's home." In the next line he tells us that Phania has already gone. Similarly, at line 502 Chremes rushes offstage to tell two friends, hitherto unmentioned, that he cannot help them in a property dispute that day. Menedemus delivers a short speech (502–7), and Chremes comes directly back, having accomplished his purpose.

Why has Terence created such situations (or allowed them to stand from Menander)? In the case of line 170 Chremes can simply walk upstage to knock on a door, and so the action need take little time, but there is no real need for him to do so. At line 502 there is a greater disruption. The content of Menedemus's short speech, to the effect that men judge the affairs of others more accurately than their own, has a deliciously ironic flavor in view of Chremes' eagerness to help someone else when he is so ignorant of his own situation; however, it is hardly important enough or long enough to warrant Chremes' interrupting the action by dashing off and on again so quickly.

Two explanations have been suggested. One might be termed positive: Terence is at pains to show Chremes as a busybody who is eager to insinuate himself into other people's affairs. Thus, he cannot simply wait for his neighbor to come over; he must go fetch him. What is more, he will happily agree to serve as an arbitrator for friends, or decide hastily to postpone this service at the prospect of becoming involved in Menedemus's affairs.[21] The second is less complimentary of Terence's technique. A persistent theory posits in the comedy of Menander and other New Comic poets the presence of a choral element, not integrated into the action as in Old Comedy, but presented at pauses in the action for spectacle. Thus, in Menander after

Chremes' exit at line 170 and after Menedemus's exit on his heels at line 507 there would have been such interludes, motivated by Chremes' movements. The presumption would be, then, that Terence was not particularly careful in reworking these passages for his own theater, which did not regularly feature such performances.[22]

An examination of the machinations of Syrus also reveals problems, as we learned in the brief comments on plot. The slave is commissioned by Chremes to find money, ostensibly for Clinia, although, of course, he is actually looking for a thousand drachmas with which to fulfill Clitipho's promise to Bacchis. He outlines a plan to the old man (598 ff.), starting with the statement that the girl Antiphila has come to Bacchis as surety on the debt made by the old Corinthian woman, who has died; perhaps Menedemus can be convinced to redeem the girl if he is told she is from a rich Carian family and can be ransomed back at a profit. A curious exchange follows (610–12):

CH: You're making a miscalculation.

SY: How so?

CH: I'll give you Menedemus's answer: "No sale." What will you do then?

SY: You're answering what I hoped.

CH: How so?

SY: There's no need.

CH: There's no need?

SY: I'll explain in a minute.

At this point they are interrupted by Sostrata with her news about Antiphila, and we are left confused as to how Menedemus's refusal can lead to Syrus's getting the money.

In fact, when Syrus had just arrived with Bacchis and Antiphila, he proposed to pass off Bacchis to Chremes as Clinia's mistress. When pressed about what to do with Antiphila, he said she should be sent to Clitipho's mother. To the question "why?" he answers, "It's a long story, Clitipho, for me to tell you why I'm doing it" (332–33). Are we to accept this as a clumsy way of putting Clitipho off? Or is it meant to foreshadow Syrus's suspicions even at this point about the girl's origins?

After Chremes and Sostrata have gone in to examine Antiphila more closely, Syrus has a short speech expressing his frustration at the turn of events. In the end, however, he seems to have found a new plan and exits with, "Great, I've got a fine idea. Yes sirree, I think I'll get back that money anyway that just flew the coop" (677–78a). It is not unprecedented in plays of slave intrigue for the schemer to give appearance of great plans which may not work out at all, but Syrus comes up singularly empty. He describes his idea to Clinia saying, "This plan takes the cake; I'm really showing myself off . . ." (709). But the plan, that they will transport Bacchis to Clinia's house and confess everything to Menedemus, has several rough edges, as Clinia points out. Syrus can only dismiss objections as carping and confesses in the end that he is really trying to create confusion so that he can stall for time.

None of his manipulations is directly responsible for acquiring the money. Instead, he follows the flow of his conversation with Chremes (749 ff.) until the old man agrees to make good on the debt for which his daughter was surety without much prodding at all (cf. 790–96). Thus, in all Syrus's bluster there has been more wind than rain. In fact, the second plan does lead to Chremes' bitter downfall (874 ff.). Chremes assures an excited Menedemus that Clinia's claims are meant only to get money on the pretense of financing wedding arrangements, because he can recognize Clinia's supposed confession as part of Syrus's trick. When the truth comes out, then, his fall is all the harder, but the slave is only accidentally the agent.

Finally, Syrus is responsible for starting the play's final sequence in motion when he spreads doubt in the frantic, disinherited Clitipho's mind about his parentage (978 ff.). Granted there is an important theme of the relationship between father and son which this total loss of confidence in the biological relationship underscores, still, this sudden development seems singularly unmotivated, even though it leads to the successful resolution of the plot.

As we have mentioned earlier, one school of critics has suggested that the prologue, which would have explained the relationships of the play to the audience in the beginning, has been omitted from Terence's version of Menander's play. An omniscient audience would have more easily followed the route of the action and thus seen the irony of some of Syrus's planning and perhaps been prepared for Syrus's curious advice to Clitipho to question his mother about his parentage.

Be that as it may, it is possible, of course, to point to clumsiness in Terence's structure without damning his whole dramaturgy in *The Self-Tormentor*.[23] As we shall see, speculation about these structural questions has led to some very useful observations about Terence's characters.

"Duality" Composition. "Duality" composition is, as we have seen, a pronounced feature of Terence's dramatic structuring. If *The Girl from Andros* presents a sort of "experiment" with duality, then, when we learn from the prologue that Terence "doubled" Menander's "simple" plot (line 6), we are naturally expectant to see the way in which he utilizes a structure which he seems at such pains to effect. If we had a commentary by Donatus as we do for the other plays, we would doubtless know far more about what Terence did to Menander's play. As it is, scholars are left to speculate. Speculation in this area, as in other aspects of the play, has been valuable in helping us to see what Terence has ultimately accomplished.

In *The Self-Tormentor* there are two love affairs, intertwined in such a way as to help to resolve each other. The interaction is not perfectly equal, for the love of Clinia and Antiphila is of considerably greater importance than the affair of Clitipho and Bacchis. Furthermore, both affairs do not end happily, since Clitipho must marry to satisfy his father and cannot simply continue with Bacchis. The Clitipho-Bacchis situation provides a background for Clinia and Antiphila, however, and it is the affair which generates the need for action that brings together not only the lovers but also the fathers and sons.

In addition to the intertwining of the love affairs, there are three sets of paired characters, Menedemus and Chremes, Clinia and Clitipho, Antiphila and Bacchis, which are used effectively to establish both characterizations and theme. All of these are given important scenes in which they interact directly with one another. For example, Menedemus and Chremes begin the play with such a scene (53 ff.); Clinia and Clitipho discuss their mistresses (230 ff.); Bacchis talks with Antiphila about the life of the courtesan and that of the devoted mistress (381 ff.). Furthermore, the other relationships, such as Menedemus-Clinia versus

Chremes-Clitipho, are related and are compared with great effect in developing the themes of the play.

Characters. In general the characterizations of *The Self-Tormentor* develop straightforwardly, and we can survey the principal figures without difficulty. Chremes offers special problems, however. An important part of the characterizations is found, of course, in comparisons and contrasts so that some of the figures are best examined together.

Clinia and Clitipho. The love affairs of Clinia and Clitipho form the foundation for the plot of *The Self-Tormentor.* Therefore, as one might expect from the play's duality construction, the characters of the two men can be seen best in comparison and contrast. Despite the prominent place of their affairs in the plot, however, neither character is particularly remarkable.

Of the two, Clinia is the less interesting. Although much energy is expended to solve his problems, we see little of him. We are meant to think well of him, surely, as a young man whose heart has brought him into conflict with his father, but whose courage has sent him off to prove that he is worthy of respect. As old Chremes says, it is the undertaking of a "respectful and energetic spirit" (120). Yet our first view of him is not so favorable, for we find him tormented with suspicion that his Antiphila has been corrupted by offers from other suitors. Clitipho's comparison of her to Bacchis (223 ff.) has left us with the impression of a mistress so devoted that she is undeserving of Clinia's doubts. That he voices them helps to establish his youthful confusion. Apart from this concern, however, his devotion to Antiphila is complete, and he rushes to marry her at the earliest opportunity.

In contrast to his friend, Clitipho exhibits a somewhat richer character. On the one hand, he is the typical young lover in the grasp of a courtesan devoted to taking his money. On the other, his warm concern for his young friend is evident from his conversation with Chremes in which he reports Clinia's presence (175 ff.). He is meditative enough to deliver such lines, albeit they are thoroughly sententious, as "if I ever have a son, let him find me gentle. There'll be the opportunity of both finding out about and of forgiving a mistake" (217–18); it is he who has the amusing interchange with Chremes after he has been caught fondling Bacchis, and so must go off grumbling, sent on a walk by Syrus to keep him out of trouble (562 ff.).

His most touching traits are seen, however, in his scene with Syrus where he exhibits utter despair at his father's disinheriting him (978 ff.). His confusion underscores the lack of true understanding that exists between him and Chremes, so that Syrus's suggestion that he doubt his parentage takes hold of him immediately. Despite the peculiarity of Syrus's advice, the scene is effective in enlisting our sympathy: young men of Clitipho's stripe are not as a rule dissolute, only a bit indulged, or undersupervised.[24] All that has gone before suggests to us that Chremes' response is too harsh, and it is important that Clitipho's character is such that his abject confusion so moves us.

Syrus. Syrus is the slave in Terence most nearly approximating the traditional *servus callidus,* or "tricky slave," of Roman comedy. Davus in *The Girl from Andros* and Syrus in *The Brothers* help their young masters to a certain extent, but only Syrus's role is devoted almost entirely to tricking his master's father. Once his stock attributes are established, however, his character becomes rather unremarkable. He has some fine scenes for acting, such as his interchanges with the two young men while awaiting the women's arrival, where he surprises Clitipho with the news that Bacchis is on her way, or his handling of Clitipho after that young man has been discovered with his hand in Bacchis's dress, and his subsequent exchange with Chremes when his master ironically gives him permission to engage in all manner of trickery. Throughout, however, his character maintains a straightforward adherence to the role of comic trickster and shows little variety or development.

Antiphila and Bacchis. Like their male counterparts, Antiphila and Bacchis are characterized by comparison. They are, of course, drawn as opposites, and that contrast establishes basic stereotypes. Neither has a big part, and their simplicity keeps the relationships clear-cut.

Antiphila's portrayal rests on her one scene in which she talks briefly with Bacchis and then rushes into Clinia's arms (381 ff.), but we know a good deal about her from what others, especially Clitipho and Syrus, say. She is devoted, chaste, and self-denying. Bacchis, on the other hand, is a hardheaded business woman, who knows she must make her fortune before her attractiveness fades. She has another scene (723 ff.) in which she shows her colors, manipulating Syrus easily and exciting him to new activity to find her promised money with threats of a defection to another lover. She too, however, is characterized by reports, especially from Clitipho and Chremes, which establish her powers of consumption and her demanding nature. In the end neither of the women rises above her stereotype.

Sostrata.   Sostrata is a genuinely interesting minor character. She is a type of comic wife not often found, neither a carping henpeck nor a submissive cipher. She is developed by two scenes, both with Chremes (614 ff. and 1003 ff.). In the first, when she confesses that she did not expose the daughter born to them many years before, but, despite Chremes' instructions, turned the task over to someone else, we see in her both a sense of deference expected in a Roman matron and the genuine humanity of a young mother faced with the exposure of her child.

Her straightforward humanity contrasts markedly with Chremes' reaction to her report. He lectures her on the impropriety of her actions and generally takes a superior tone, quite in keeping with his character. In the next scene, however, it is Sostrata who shows the stronger hand. Clitipho comes to her with his pathetic concerns for his parentage, following Chremes' disowning him, and she is instrumental in forcing her husband into a more balanced position. In sum, for such a small role Terence has provided considerable richness of character.

Chremes and Menedemus.   The focus of attention in a given play of Terence tends to be on one element, either embodied in a character or as a single thematic issue. It is to this element that other features converge to develop the play's characters, action, and themes. In *The Self-Tormentor* the key figure is Chremes.

Chremes' concern for Menedemus puts the play in motion, and his lack of perceptiveness about Clitipho leads to the complex of actions in Syrus's trickery, as well as the play's final resolution. Thus, it is his character that provides the perspective for the play's principal ironies: Chremes is so full of advice for Menedemus and so in need of advice himself. Menedemus, for example, thinks he is talking about himself, but his remarks fit Chremes much better when he says, "This is the way of human nature: men see and dispose of other people's business better than their own" (503–5). Or, consider the broad irony of Chremes' exhortations to Syrus that a young man's slave should help in exceptional cases to trick his father (511 ff.).

At the beginning it is Menedemus who seems to need help to moderate his reaction to Clinia's leaving home. By the end of the play Chremes must be helped to acclimate himself to the realization that his actions toward Clitipho have been too harsh.

A key issue is Chremes' motivation. Early in the play he says, in response to Menedemus's question about why he has interposed himself into his affairs, "I am a human being: I think nothing pertaining to humanity out of my range of concern" (77). That single line has been the center of the debate: is Chremes a concerned humanitarian or a self-satisfied busybody?[25]

In fact, it seems important to realize that he is a little of both. His concern for Menedemus is genuine, and his interest in people seems motivated by honest caring. He is, however, very sure of himself, and easily slides into self-satisfaction. He can lecture Menedemus on the need to communicate with children and treat them with understanding, but goes into a veritable tantrum when he discovers Clitipho's involvement with Bacchis.

Menedemus, by contrast, is less complicated. He wins our sympathy easily, eager as he is to make amends for his mistake and to admit the shortcomings of his understanding. He seems submissive and easily led, for his confusion has played on his confidence; he is not by nature weak, but comes to Chremes out of that confusion. After submitting to Chremes' dictates, he is understandably pleased to be able to puncture Chremes' pomposity with the news about his son. Still, when it is necessary to curb Chremes' excess, Menedemus gives as good as he has received and adds his voice to Sostrata's in an effort to reconcile father and son. His is a thoroughly humane and likeable character, of moral substance, but without great complexity.

With Menedemus's relatively straightforward character in mind, we must return to Chremes. The issue of whether he is humanitarian or busybody turns on several points. Those who would caution against our taking a too high opinion of him cite his eagerness to insert himself into everyone's business: he cannot wait for his neighbor to come to dinner, but goes to remind him; he must postpone a commitment to help two acquaintances as an arbitrator in a boundary dispute in order to involve himself in Menedemus's affairs; his son Clitipho pictures him as always offering advice, largely undigested by his bored child (214 ff.); he is consistently giving highly sententious observations on all manner of subjects. On the other side, we might argue that he is pictured as eager to be helpful; that sons frequently think their fathers preachy; that sententious advice is frequently sound, despite its triteness.

Two other events are more difficult to counter. Chremes' treatment of Sostrata is not marked by the same consideration he gives to others. It is much more the stock reaction of the comic husband to his spouse. We may therefore disqualify it as evidence of serious character development, but it remains behavior more compatible with a less rather than more genuinely humane character. Finally, his reaction to Clitipho's unexpected involvement with Bacchis may well be taken as the last step in the exposure of his true nature. The only explanation consistent with the more favorable view of the character must be that he is taking decisive steps to bring Clitipho into line, and that his harshness is a ploy, never a real expression of feeling.[26] The solution to the problem of Chremes' characterization may lie ultimately in the hands of the director, who must either create in us enough sympathy for Chremes to be viewed kindly in the face of the play's irony, or bring his character methodically to his final, ironic unveiling. In the end Chremes' role is the most significant single element in the play.

Theme. *The Self-Tormentor* exhibits two intertwined themes: the relationship between father and son, a common Terentian concern, and self-knowledge versus self-ignorance. It is a feature of duality composition that these themes do interlock, and their presentation develops chiefly from the comparisons inherent in the pairs of characters. These themes also lead us to speculation about some more general issues, namely, the extent to which the play is indicative of a Menandrian, and generally Hellenistic, outlook rather than one espoused actively by Terence, and the extent to which the play may seem more philosophical than it is in actuality because of the many sententious passages, which were a special feature of Menander's expression.

The ironic development of the father-son motif is a markedly successful feature of the play. Menedemus is the father outwardly repentant at his lack of success in dealing with his son; Clinia is the son who leaves a mistress to whom he is genuinely devoted in order to try to please his father. Chremes seeks to ameliorate this situation, while he is unaware of the need for concern in his own relationship with his son.

Thus the relationship between Menedemus and Clinia ultimately emphasizes at once their need for better communication to express their mutual affection and the irony of Chremes' assumption that he is well qualified to lecture on child rearing. Chremes becomes a prototype for the self-assured and self-satisfied individual whose concern for others does not make him extraordinarily sensitive to his own situation. In fact, Menedemus' comment on man's ability to see the affairs of others more clearly than his own (503–5) could be cited as a fair statement of this theme.

These thematic concerns in *The Self-Tormentor* can be seen in the light of a conscious interest in individual action of the sort often found in philosophical movements such as Stoicism and Epicureanism popular during the Hellenistic period. It has been argued that Menander's drama was influenced by such concerns.[27] Thus the much-discussed line 77 ("I am a human being: I think nothing pertaining to humanity out of my range of concern") has often been cited as Terence's retention of that philosophical concern and personal commitment to it. Indeed, the play's greatest strength ultimately lies in the depth of genuine feeling exhibited by the characters for each other and the clarification of their ironic shortcomings through the action of the plot. But *The Self-Tormentor* is not really a philosophical drama, for there is no specific philosophical program which it propounds. It is possible to argue, therefore, that the philosophical tone that appears to mark the piece is the result more of the pithy, but sententious lines spoken by many of the characters from Chremes to Menedemus to Clitipho than from a carefully structured program.

The issue is of keen interest to those who seek an understand-

ing of Terence from the biographical information that has come
down to us. Early on he was connected with the Scipio family.
That family led a political faction noted in part for its eagerness
to bring to Rome the culture of the Hellenistic world. We know,
for example, that the Stoic philosopher Panaetius (ca. 185–109
B.C.) found a ready patron in Scipio Aemilianus when he came
to Rome around 144 B.C. It is not a great leap to think of
Scipio as interested in philosophy from youth and to postulate
a mutual interest therein as one of the bases of his relationship
with Terence. We have seen elsewhere, however, the need for
great care in using the Terentian biography in interpretation
(cf. the discussions in chap. 1).

In the final analysis one can say that the themes of *The Self-
Tormentor* do stand out. It is not an oppressively preachy play,
but it does explore effectively, in the manner which is so typical
of New Comedy, important questions of human behavior and
man's relationships.

The Eunuch (*Eunuchus*)

Plot.   The play opens with a conversation between a young
Athenian, Phaedria, and his slave Parmeno. Phaedria is deeply
involved with a courtesan, Thais, and is afraid that she has grown
cool toward him in order to accommodate another lover. He
resolves to be firm with her, but when Thais makes her appearance, she quickly masters him with her flattering manner and
a story about a young girl. This girl, Pamphila, was brought
to Thais's mother at Rhodes by a trader who bought her from
robbers that had stolen her near Athens. She was raised in the
house virtually as Thais's sister. Thais moved from her home
to Athens with a lover, who died and left her with her present
establishment. She became involved with a soldier, Thraso, immediately before her present affair with Phaedria, who left Athens on business in the east. Thais's mother recently died, and
her uncle, unsympathetic to the girl's special place in the household, put her up for sale. Thraso happened to be in Rhodes,
bought Pamphila, and has returned to Athens with her as a
present for Thais. Thais believes that she can restore the girl
to her family and thereby gain support in the community. Thraso
has taken umbrage, however, at Thais's involvement with Phaed-

ria and threatens to withhold his gift. Therefore, Thais begs Phaedria to go to his family's country house for two days so that she can deal with the soldier. Charmed, if frustrated, Phaedria agrees, giving instructions to Parmeno before he goes to bring his own gifts to Thais, an Ethiopian serving girl and a eunuch.

The action continues with the entrance of Gnatho, a professional hanger-on, or "parasite," who is bringing Pamphila to Thais. He introduces himself with a long, humorous discourse on his clever practice of the "parasite" profession. He meets Parmeno, and the two exchange insults. Gnatho has the girl, an impressive gift, and so he has the better of the exchange and enters Thais's house in triumph.

As Parmeno grouses over the situation, Chaerea, Phaedria's younger brother, comes rushing onstage. He has seen a young girl on the street, been immediately smitten by her, and pursued her, only to lose sight of her when forced to exchange conversation with an old family friend. Parmeno informs him that she has been brought to Thais's house. In the course of listening to Chaerea declare his ardor, the slave observes, jokingly, that if Chaerea were the eunuch, whom Phaedria has bought for Thais, he could be near his love to his heart's content. Chaerea picks up the idea and forces Parmeno to allow him to change places with the eunuch.

As they exit, Thraso and Gnatho enter. Their conversation reveals the crass stupidity of Thraso. Thais appears, and as the three talk, Parmeno enters with the serving girl and Chaerea dressed as the eunuch. He now scores points against Thraso and Gnatho by displaying the quality of his gifts with the cultured Chaerea posing as the eunuch. Preparing to leave with Thraso, Thais gives instructions concerning the new arrivals and instructs her slave Pythias to deal with Chremes, whom she believes to be the girl's brother, if he arrives in her absence. Chremes does arrive. He gives an account of Thais's previous interview with him and his suspicions of her motives. Pythias cannot convince him to return, or to wait, so she takes him to Thais at Thraso's.

Enter Antipho, a friend, who is looking for Chaerea. Chaerea exits Thais's house at this moment very excited. He eagerly relates to Antipho the story of his adventures in the house:

after being admitted, he was put in charge of watching over the girl; when the maids had withdrawn after helping her bathe and groom, they were left alone; struck by the felicity of this opportunity, he took his pleasure of the girl, and immediately ran outside. The two resolve to return to Antipho's house so that Chaerea can change clothes.

Thais's slave Dorias enters with her mistress's jewelry, sent ahead for fear that an argument is brewing with Thraso. Phaedria also enters, having decided after all not to stay in the country. These two are met by Pythias, who comes from the house with the report of the rape. The two maids confront Phaedria with the eunuch's transgression; he goes into his house and produces the real eunuch. Upon investigation Chaerea's deception is made clear, and Phaedria exits in confusion while the maids conspire to keep the situation from Thais.

Chremes enters, followed closely by Thais. We learn about the imbroglio with Thraso, and Thais tells Chremes of her belief that Pamphila is his sister and her plan to bring in the child's old nurse to identify some childhood trinkets. The two await the arrival of Thraso.

There follows a scene of broad farce in which Thraso, egged on by Gnatho, brings in an "army" of assorted household slaves in order to take back the girl. He arrays his troops, retreats to their rear, and calls on Thais to give back his gift. He is no match for her, however, and eventually retreats in disorder, confused in part by claims that Pamphila is an Athenian citizen.

Thais learns of the rape and berates Pamphila generally. They see Chaerea, still dressed as the eunuch, returning from his friend's house, where he had found the parents home so that he was not able to change. Thais confronts him, and, although initially brash, he suddenly professes his love for Pamphila and puts himself in Thais's hands. They go inside, but Pythias, disgusted that the offender should be pardoned so easily, resolves to have some revenge on Parmeno at least. She convinces him that Chaerea has been seized, trussed, and threatened with castration as punishment for raping an Athenian citizen. At this moment Chaerea's father arrives from the country, and Parmeno tells him the story. The two rush into Thais's house, and the maid returns luxuriating in her triumph.

Thraso and Gnatho return, for the soldier has decided to

humble himself before Thais. The other principals come from her house, and we learn that Chaerea is betrothed to Pamphila, that Thais has come under the protection of his father, and that Phaedria's place with her is secure. Gnatho, however, is able to convince Phaedria that he should allow Thraso access to Thais because he is rich enough to pay the bills for all and foolish enough to be of no threat as a true rival. On this note the play ends.

The plot of *The Eunuch* is surely Terence's most sprightly. As we will see, several features in its structure have been the subject of critical examination. The play, however, was his most successful. An immediate hit, it doubtless secured Terence's place on the Roman stage.

Structure.   The structure of *The Eunuch* has been the subject of a great deal of comment, much more than one might expect from a play with a rather straightforward plot. Terence's prologue has provided the springboard for much speculation because from it (30–33) we learn that two characters, Gnatho, the meal-cadger, or toady (Latin: *parasitus,* hence, "parasite"), and Thraso, the boastful soldier (*miles gloriosus*), were taken from Menander's *The Flatterer* (*Colax*) and worked into Terence's rendition of his *The Eunuch.* In such a circumstance scholars eager to unravel the two plays have examined Terence's structure closely to analyze its parts into distinct groups from the two sources.

The play itself has also undergone inspection: on the one hand by those who have felt that it exhibits compositional flaws, especially in the use of the two "borrowed" characters, on the other by critics who have found a subtle ordering of elements to move toward the conclusion of a theme which has been developing throughout. For one group *The Eunuch* is Terence's farcical bow to popular taste and financial success, for the other it is a play quite in keeping with its author's general tendencies and techniques.

"Duality" Construction.   In *The Eunuch* Terence employs his favorite double-style plot. Whether he found it in Menander or fashioned it himself, as in *The Self-Tormentor,* is not altogether clear; in either case, this is not an especially notable example of duality composition. The two affairs, those of Phaedria and his brother Chaerea, are not connected from the start, but become entwined only by accident. Thus, the close connection of the fate of one affair with that of the other is not a major issue, though in the end they are resolved together, when Chaerea is betrothed to Pamphila and Phaedria's position with Thais is made secure by his father's becoming her protector.

Nor does the play make especially careful use of paired characters, a feature of duality structure. As we will see, the characters on the whole are not remarkable. Some effect is achieved by the sharp contrast between Phaedria, the hesitant, pusillanimous young lover, and Chaerea, the impetuous suitor. In addition, the slave Parmeno is contrasted with two characters through his competition with Gnatho and, more significantly, by his interactions with Thais's maid, Pythias.

The Roles of Gnatho and Thraso. The effectiveness of Terence's use of the parasite and the soldier has been one of the chief points of controversy in evaluating *The Eunuch*. Some of the interest has been of a literary-historical nature, as we have seen often in criticism of Terence's plays: did Terence make a fundamental change in Menander's play with the additions, or was he substituting different characters for roughly parallel roles; especially, what sort of rival for the courtesan was in Menander's *The Eunuch*?[28] Such questions have not, of course, been answered definitively. Donatus helps us to some extent, but is not a decisive aid—we know, for example, that Terence made such structural changes as the introduction of young Antipho (549 ff.) so that Chaerea could tell his story of rape in dialogue form rather than in monologue as in Menander, but he is of less help on Gnatho and Thraso. As usual, these discussions are most helpful to us as a means of focusing on potential problem areas in the play's structure.

In fact, the critical issue can be simply put: are Gnatho and Thraso intrusive elements whose chief function is farce, or have they been worked skillfully into the dramatic structure?[29] Examination of two scenes will serve to illustrate the point.

The first is the interchange between Gnatho and Parmeno (232 ff.), which begins actually with Gnatho's monologue on his life-style (232–65). Gnatho's reason for being onstage is to deliver Thraso's gift, the young girl Pamphila, to Thais. The content of his long speech has nothing to do with the subject at hand, and, since Gnatho is a stock character, no long characterization is necessary. Thus, a purist may criticize Terence's scene as having inorganic elements. Gnatho's long speech can be seen as an example of a general weakness in the use of the character in that surface comedy does not contribute to the internal dynamics of the action. Therefore, Terence has been accused of yielding to the temptation to introduce a humorous character for its own sake.

There are, of course, counterarguments at hand. One might argue that the purist is too prescriptive in demanding that there must be so close a melding of humor and purpose. The first business of comedy is entertainment, so that a more appropriate criterion might be the "playability" of the scene, not its adherence to some theory of composition. A better defense of Terence, however, is that Gnatho's role is important to the overall structure of the play, as is his long speech. We will see in our section on theme that a cogent argument can be made that the "philosophy" expounded in the speech is important to the development of the play's theme, and that Gnatho's role in general is an important element in the presentation of that theme.[30]

A second example is the "battle scene" (771–816), perhaps the best-known segment in the play. Here Thraso arrives at Thais's door, angry that Chremes was introduced to their party. He is demanding his present back, and he has brought an "army" of household slaves with which to assault Thais's house. Again, the purist may object that the scene interrupts the action for far too long without furthering the plot. We know already that Thraso is a blowhard and undercompetent without having to be shown it by his handling of the "battle." Thus, this scene, like so much of the soldier's part, finds its chief *raison d'être* in its farcical humor.

The counterarguments are much the same as before. The action is rich enough to stand on its own. Furthermore, it does allow for some character development which is useful to the final purpose of the play. The depth of Thraso's commitment to Thais is a significant motivation for his actions at the play's end. The timidity of Chremes is an important detail: he is far from being the stalwart defender of his long-lost sister. Finally,

Thais's control over all the men in the play is established all the more clearly by her sweeping rout of Thraso's battle plan.

The Conclusion of *The Eunuch*.   Questions of moral conduct must inevitably arise in discussing a play such as *The Eunuch*. These are more closely related to character (What must we think of a young man who would rape the girl of his dreams in clear conscience?) and theme (Is the play meant in some way to explore moral conduct?). The moral issue is important to a discussion of structure, however, because of the play's last scene.[31]

Many have found the arrangement negotiated by Gnatho, in which Thraso is to be accepted as a "rival" by Phaedria, offensive and indicative of the play's structural weaknesses. It is not really a question of conduct, although one might be personally bothered by the callous arrangement. The question is rather why Terence needed to bring Thraso back at all. Certainly the ending neatly settles all accounts, but Phaedria began the play very concerned about the soldier as a rival. It seems on the surface a rather contrived solution that he should consent in his moment of victory to allow him access to Thais simply because he is a rich dolt who can finance an expensive mistress for them both and never be a serious rival for her affections.

Several explanations might be put forward. The most obvious is that this sort of conclusion was well founded in the tradition (cf. Plautus's *The Twin Sisters Bacchis* and *The Ass-Comedy*). There is, in fact, comic theory to support this device in the form, for example, of Frye's "blocking character" who at the end of a play is integrated back into the community.[32] As often with the "Gnatho-Thraso" problem, however, the strongest defense of Terence's craftsmanship can be found in an explanation that relates to the play's overall theme: it is important to see that Thraso is brought back, and callously used, as a means of underscoring finally the true nature of the young men. Phaedria and Chaerea are quick to speak of higher feelings of devotion when referring to their loves. It is Thraso, however, who cares enough for Thais to want her on any terms, and the young men are callous enough to pursue self-interest before romance.[33]

Characters.   The characters of *The Eunuch* are principally stock figures. Their individuation is generally less pronounced than in other plays of Terence, and yet this play contains some of his most memorable roles. In fact, Donatus does us a service in reminding us that the three principal roles are Parmeno, Chaerea, and Phaedria, for Thais, Gnatho, and Thraso are the ones who stand out in our minds. The playwright's most particularized creation is not one of these major roles, however, but the role of Thais's maid Pythias. Although they are primarily stock figures, the characters are worthy of some closer examination.

The Young Men: Phaedria, Chremes, Chaerea.   Phaedria is a typical young lover whose mistress is a practicing courtesan. In accord with the model of his type, he is reliant on his slave for support, though in this play there is no plot to gain money for his affair. He is indecisive in his emotions and how to face up to his mistress. Despite the difference in their social standings, he has affection for Thais, and there is nothing tawdry in their liaison. On the whole, he is a positive character, but lacking in any strength and hence easily led to the bargain with which the play ends.

Chaerea offers an effective contrast to his brother. He comes on stage (293) with an energy that seems all the more dynamic in comparison with his brother's indecision. In fact, quick, even mercurial, action marks him throughout. He has also a somewhat richer character than his brother. We must, of course, place in some sort of perspective his rape of Pamphila. It is in part the result of his overall impetuosity, the volatile temperament that leads to a betrothal by late afternoon. Thus he is saved in our opinion by his formulaic qualities, and by the fact that convention assures us the girl's honor will be vindicated by marriage. But he cannot be completely absolved, even in terms of the play. In his encounter with Thais (840 ff.), which ends in reconciliation with the courtesan, he begins with a flippant attitude. He can refer to his deed as "a little something" (856) and excuse his actions on grounds that he thought he was dealing with "a fellow slave" (858). In the end it is important that we neither try to paint him black nor to absolve him completely: he is shown to us as an acceptable husband for Pamphila, but a basically selfish young man used to the run of the town.

Chremes' role is slight, but he is onstage enough to establish one trait. He has considerable timidity. From his anxiety about falling into some sort of trap at Thais's hands (515 ff.) to Thais's aggravation at his fear of facing Thraso ("My god, this man I've put forth as my defender needs someone to take care of him!" [770]), he is shown as cautious and concerned first about his personal welfare, a fact of significance when one remembers that ostensibly he has come to rescue his lost sister from ignominy.

Thais.   Thais is a stock type, the kindly courtesan, found in other plays of New Comedy—Bacchis of Terence's *The Mother-in-Law* is another example. Instead of the grasping, aggressive personality of many other comic prostitutes, this type is genuinely sensitive to the feelings of those with whom she deals. Thais is, for example, sincerely fond of Phaedria and happy at the end of the play to be able to devote herself to him. It is important, however, to see that Terence has not romanticized her in this role. She is a thoroughgoing professional who is quite capable of playing off one patron against another. Nor should we forget that the welfare of her "sister" is not her first concern in uniting Pamphila with her family. She is eager to make more secure her own place in the community through an act of kindness to an Athenian citizen. When she chastises Chaerea, she is careful to say, ". . . You have so thwarted my plans that I cannot turn her over to her relatives as was right and as I was eager to do so that I could garner firm goodwill for myself, Chaerea" (868–71).

Finally, in this play filled with men, Thais is clearly in control of all situations: Phaedria is putty in her hands; Chremes succumbs to her blandishments; Thraso retreats before her; Chaerea entrusts himself completely to her. Although she wants to secure the patronage of a solid citizen, her competence stands in sharp contrast to the confusion of the other characters.

Gnatho, Parmeno, Thraso.   Gnatho and Parmeno are placed in contrastive opposition, the difference in their social standings notwithstanding. Parmeno, we must remember from Donatus, is the play's chief role. He is onstage throughout to support his young masters, though he is not the "tricky slave" of the type played by Syrus in *The Self-Tormentor.* He supports Phaedria in his affair, however, and, ironically, provides the idea to Chaerea of exchanging places with the eunuch. As a character somewhat stronger than the young men he represents, he shows some spunk in dealing with Thais (cf. 98 ff.), and he is eager to defend the family honor against Gnatho and the soldier. His finest moment comes when he can pay Gnatho back for the parasite's highhandedness at the delivery of Pamphila by bringing the cultured Chaerea as a eunuch to Thais (454 ff.).

Gnatho's is a fine character role. We have seen already the disagreement over the effectiveness with which he and Thraso are employed in the play's structure. As a character, however, he is a typical stock parasite. He stands in relation to Thraso as Parmeno does to Phaedria and Chaerea, and spars with the slave to establish his wit and cleverness. And, of course, he consistently underscores Thraso's obvious crassness to insure that no laughable foible is missed.

Thraso, too, is a thoroughly stock type, modified just enough, however, to make his character function properly in establishing the play's theme. He is consistently shown as an unreflective, crass blowhard and a rather poor excuse for a soldier. The "battle scene" (771 ff.) is the climax of this characterization, where Thraso, directing his "troops" from a safe spot in the rear, is easily "repulsed" by Thais. Despite his obvious faults, however, the last scene makes clear his real devotion to Thais. He becomes more pathetic than ludicrous, and it is important that he be so recognized in order to understand better the implications of his treatment.

Pythias. Pythias's role is the play's really fine creation, despite its minor part in the plot. Whereas other characters operate very much within the parameters of their stock associations, Pythias is developed more individualistically, to great effect for the play's theme.

She is from the start established as an important member of Thais's household, for she is entrusted with the care of Pamphila and is instructed how to deal with Chremes in Thais's absence. With the rape of Pamphila, however, she comes into her own as a character, for she is instrumental in expressing the general outrage at the deed and in discovering its perpetrator. From this point she assumes the role of avenger, and this is an important function. When, for example, Chaerea casually remarks that he was only dealing with a fellow slave, she flies into a rage:

PY: Fellow slave! I can barely keep from pulling out his hair,
      the monster. Besides he's even come to make fun of us.

TH: Won't you get away from here, you madwoman?

PY: Why? Sure, I'd be liable, I suppose, if I did something to
      this scoundrel, especially since he's admitted to being your
      slave! (859–63)

Furthermore, her outrage does not end with Chaerea's reconciliation. What she cannot do to the master she can to the man,
so that we see her concoct an ingenious story of Chaerea being
punished for his deed, which she sells to Parmeno and he in
turn to Chaerea's father.

   Pythias, then, acquires a significance far beyond what might
be expected for her. She, not Parmeno, becomes heir to the
trickster's part. Furthermore, she performs the very important
function of acting as the play's conscience. She bears the burden
of being outraged at Chaerea for all of us. Her vengeance on
Parmeno, and her fictitious description of Chaerea's impending
castration, help to provide an outlet that can defuse some of
the normal revulsion at Chaerea's act so that it will not dominate
the play too much.

   Theme.   *The Eunuch* has divided critics quite remarkably
on the question of theme. A reading of the other plays will
lead one to expect from Terence a rather high moral tone and
clearly expressed themes on such matters as child rearing and
interpersonal relationships. This play, however, is marked much
more obviously by action than by theme—we would think
of it as *motoria* without Donatus's dutiful note on its type of
plot.

   This special quality has caused some critics to treat the play
with condescension. We have seen how its characters are somewhat more farcical than those of other plays; it was also a great
financial success. Thus, some have felt that it was a clear attempt
to curry popular favor at the expense of Terence's more usual
concern for higher issues. Norwood, who stands as the prototype
of such criticism, speaks of "Plautine" elements of the play,
and this is not for him a term of compliment. If the play is
directed at good pace, and the stock elements of character and
plot, as well as the farcical humor, are made to dominate the

stage, *The Eunuch* can reasonably be a farce without any particular theme. On the other hand, some critics have found in it a subtlety of workmanship leading to a significant theme quite in keeping with what we might expect from the rest of Terence's work.[34]

Any discussion of theme must confront immediately the moral tone of the play. It is not enough to dismiss those features which we would today find morally objectionable by citing differences in attitudes between the centuries, or to plead a special code of conduct for a young gentleman in a brothel. Rape under a variety of circumstances is a feature of New Comedy, and rather unromantic and unsavory arrangements are made among gentlemen with respect to a practicing courtesan. Roman comedy (and its descendants) is not the genre for those who object to these features out of hand. But we are dealing here with the callous rape of a young girl by a swain who is professing instant devotion, not a drunken act against an anonymous subject. Furthermore, one has a right to question an ending in which Phaedria quickly accepts Thraso as a rival after he has spent so much of the play grieved at this very prospect.

In fact, we can argue for a theme developed carefully and subtly throughout the play.[35] Stated straightforwardly, the play deals with selfishness of a particular sort, and it does so in a manner quite typical of New Comedy, by showing the contrast between what characters appear to be and what they are.

Phaedria and Chaerea both talk of love as if it made them highly solicitous of someone outside themselves. Yet Phaedria cannot get beyond his own sense of discomfort in his relationship with Thais. He cannot, for example, finally grant her the two days she asks to accomplish a purpose very important to her. And in the end he is willing enough to assent to an arrangement which will make his affair as comfortable for him as possible. Chaerea is full of ardor and protestations of love, but he is above all eager to satisfy his immediate desires. His whole personality is based on a compulsive energy to gratify itself. He can, then, callously rape Pamphila, brag about it to his friend Antipho, and make light of it to Thais, only to change direction suddenly and secure his betrothal to her just as quickly as he raped her.

Thais appears to have an admirable interest in the welfare

of others, Phaedria, Chremes, Chaerea, Pamphila. All her actions are, however, fundamentally self-serving. She tempers everything she does, even her search for Pamphila's family, with concern for her position, and she uses her considerable way with men to accomplish everything she wishes.

Only Pythias among the "good" characters stands against this attitude. That is what makes her so important in the play's structure. On the one hand, she acts as an outlet for our natural emotions so that the play does not frustrate or elicit indignation at the wrong subject; moral turpitude is not the subject. On the other, she continues to remind us that we do not have to accept the action without moral objection just because we are moving in a comic stage world.

The final proof of Terence's theme, however, is found in the characters of Gnatho and Thraso. These are the figures whose effectiveness has been often questioned; they are, however, the very characters Terence was at pains to work into his play. That they provide the ultimate clarification of the theme is a tribute to his careful craftmanship.

Gnatho is a character unabashedly devoted to self-interest. His speech on "parasiting" as a trade (232 ff.) is an encomium to that life-style. His advice is simply that each man should strive for his own advantage. On the surface, this is a doctrine to be derided; when compared to other characters' motives, it seems to be the thought of the day, however. Thraso represents the other side of the coin. He is so outwardly crass and foolish that he would seem to be the last character to be taken seriously. At the end of the play, however, he is not comic but pathetic in his desire to be admitted to Thais on any terms. He is expressing the honest emotion of affection for someone outside himself. That emotion is ultimately ridiculed by the rest of the characters who take advantage of Thraso's weakness just as Chaerea has taken advantage of Pamphila or Thais of all the men around her. The last scene, then, says much more about the other characters than about Thraso.

Finally, *The Eunuch* can be seen quite clearly as a play very much in Terence's style. It treats an important theme of human weakness in a subtle, highly amusing, and effective way. Its positive qualities must have accounted at least as much for its instant success as did its simple, boisterous action.

Phormio (*Phormio*)

Plot. *Phormio* opens with a conversation between two slaves, Davus and Geta. Geta, family slave of Demipho and his son Antipho, discusses his family's situation with his acquaintance, Davus. Both Demipho and his brother Chremes have gone abroad on business. Geta has been put in charge of their sons, Antipho and his cousin Phaedria, but has not been able to control them. Phaedria has fallen in love with a young slave girl, Pamphila, owned by a local slave dealer. He has been following after the girl, accompanying her, for example, to her music lessons. One day, while he, Antipho, and Geta lounged in a local barbershop waiting for her to finish a lesson, a man came in with a story about a pitiful young girl and her maid, who were mourning the loss of the girl's mother. Despite her poverty and grief, her beauty was exceptional. Out of curiosity, the group decided to go see her, and Antipho fell madly in love at first sight. He pressed suit to make her his mistress, but found her maid adamant that the girl was an Athenian citizen and would not enter into such a relationship, but would consider a proposal of marriage. Antipho was willing, but knew his father would not approve a marriage to a dowerless girl. Phormio, an acquaintance and a young man eager for a challenge, came to his aid. Being versed in the law, he proposed a scheme to make it seem that Antipho was forced into the marriage by an Athenian statute that required an orphaned citizen to be married by her next of kin. He brought suit on the girl's behalf, alleging Antipho as the next of kin; Antipho's part was to offer no defense, and so he was held liable to marry the girl, Phanium. Thus, both the young men have become romantically entangled so that they and Geta await the return of the fathers with trepidation.

The slaves go their separate ways, Geta to the harbor to seek news of Demipho, who has been expected. The two young cousins enter, discussing their problems. Phaedria is envious of Antipho's marriage; Antipho would face the slave dealer who owns Pamphila rather than his father's reaction to his own marriage. They are interrupted by Geta, who reports Demipho's arrival. Antipho fearfully plans his response when he must face his father, as Phaedria and Geta offer advice, but when they see Demipho in the distance, he loses heart and runs away, calling on Phaedria and Geta to plead for him.

Demipho enters in a rage because he has learned the particulars of Antipho's marriage. He confronts Phaedria and Geta, since Antipho is not present himself, with questions about his son's conduct: why was no defense offered; why was no dowry given as an alternative, as allowed under the law, to marriage with an unknown, poverty-stricken girl. Phaedria offers explanations, Geta excuses, but Demipho will not be quieted, so they go to bring Phormio to talk with the old man. Demipho goes to find some friends to witness the interview.

Phormio and Geta return and meet Demipho and three acquaintances. Phormio thwarts Demipho's efforts to reopen the matter with a combination of legal argument and bluster and departs, leaving Demipho to consult his friends to no conclusion. The old man resolves to await the expected return of his brother Chremes and to consult him about the best course of action.

Now Antipho returns, angry at his own cowardice in leaving his affairs to his cousin. He meets Geta, who has been left onstage, and they are immediately interrupted by Phaedria and Dorio, the slave dealer who owns Pamphila, as the two exit Dorio's establishment arguing. Dorio has arranged to sell Pamphila to a soldier, since Phaedria has been unable to find the money to buy her himself. The three convince him to sell her to Phaedria if he can find the money before the soldier arrives on the next day. The two youths convince Geta to take on the task of finding the 3,000 drachmas necessary for the purchase. He agrees on condition he can enlist Phormio's help to bilk Demipho out of the money.

Demipho enters on their exit in conversation with his brother Chremes, who has just arrived from Lemnos. The two are talking about a wife and daughter who had left Lemnos before Chremes arrived there, presumably to look for him in Athens. Illness delayed his own return. It becomes obvious that Chremes has had a secret life on Lemnos, apparently known to his brother but not to his wife and son. He is disturbed to hear of Antipho's marriage, for he had hoped to marry his Lemnian daughter to her cousin so that he would not have to expose his secret to a son-in-law not so closely connected to him.

Geta returns after his strategy meeting with Phormio to find the two old men talking. He immediately executes their plan by telling Demipho that he has learned from Phormio that he would be willing to marry Phanium, and so allow the annulment of Antipho's marriage, if a dowry were offered sufficient to recompense him for renouncing an engagement already arranged at a good dowry; he is interested in finding a suitable match so that he can pay debts totaling some 3,000 drachmas. Demipho is outraged at the amount, but Chremes stands willing to give 2,000 drachmas, and to forward the entire amount immediately from the rents on his wife's estates which he has brought back from Lemnos. They agree that it is best to buy Phormio off in this fashion.

When the old men go in to fetch the money, Antipho, who has been listening to the conversation from the doorway, rushes up to Geta terrified at the arrangement. Geta assures him that it is all part of the scheme and sends him away to report their success to Phaedria. The old men return with the money. They then agree that Demipho should go to Chremes' wife, Nausistrata, and ask her to break the news of the annulment to Phanium, after he and Geta pay Phormio. They exit, but before Chremes can leave, he sees Sophrona, Phanium's maid, coming from Demipho's house. From her Chremes learns the fate of his Lemnian family, as well as the news that Phanium is married to Antipho. He rushes in to see his daughter.

Demipho and Geta return from their task. The old man goes to get Nausistrata, and the slave goes into the house. Demipho and his sister-in-law return, with her complaining of Chremes' handling of her Lemnian accounts since her father's death. They met Chremes, who tells them that he has learned new information which makes him feel that the marriage should not be annulled. Demipho is shocked at this development, but Nausistrata is pleased, for she likes the girl. As soon as they are alone, Chremes explains the situation to his brother, and they realize they must find Phormio to ask for the dowry back.

Just then Phormio himself wanders onstage fresh from helping Phaedria buy and free his young mistress. He is looking for the old men so that he can make excuses to put off the wedding. He finds Antipho instead, and the two are met by an excited Geta, who has overheard Chremes talking with Phanium. They send Antipho to her and await the return of the two old men.

Demipho and Chremes enter. There follows a heated exchange, in which Phormio first threatens lawsuits, then resorts to blackmail. Demipho is outraged and orders his slave to seize Phormio, whose cries brings Nausistrata from the house, and the whole story comes out. She is so angry that she will not consider reconciliation with Chremes until she talks to Phaedria, but takes Phormio under her protection and invites him to dinner as the play ends.

Phormio is one of Terence's "active" (*motoria*) pieces. Although its action appears complicated when summarized, it moves smoothly so that perhaps more than any other of his plays *Phormio* relies on plot ahead of other dramatic elements to achieve its success.[36] Terence has orchestrated love affairs, legal maneuvers, double lives, argumentative confrontations, and double dealings with great dramatic force and clarity.

Structure.   *Phormio* exhibits the "duality" structure found in several plays, in its two love affairs and several pairs of characters. There are also features, such as the use of legal maneuvering, that are worthy of comment. By and large, however, the structure of the play is straightforward and merits little special analysis.

We know that Terence modelled his play on *The Claimant* (*Epidicazomenos*) of Apollodorus of Carystus. He seems to have stayed unusually close to his model in this play so that scholars may have been presented an especially good opportunity to see the work of a virtually lost Greek dramatist.[37] Thus, the relationship of Terence's structure to his model, an issue in every play, may be discussed with unusual urgency in the case of *Phormio.*

"Duality" Structure.   Terence's use of duality construction, a feature of *The Self-Tormentor, The Eunuch,* and *The Brothers* as well as of *Phormio,* varies from play to play. For those who accept the traditional dating of the plays, the neat way in which the affairs of the two youths are interwoven so as to solve one another in *Phormio* indicates Terence's increasing skill in dramatic construction.[38] Although we cannot be dogmatic about the chronology for his plays, certainly duality is an outstanding feature of Terence's play.

The fates of the two young men are tied closely from the point at which they are assigned the same guardian, Geta, in their fathers' absences. The slave tells the story to his friend Davus (71 ff.): Phaedria first became involved with a slave girl who took lyre lessons, and it was while waiting for her to complete her lesson that Antipho heard the story of Phanium's sad condition. Phormio engineered Antipho's marriage, then used the marriage as part of a ploy to get the money to buy Phaedria's love, Pamphila.

In addition to the interconnections of plot, the characters are developed in pairs. Phaedria and Antipho complement each other, each eager to help the other. Demipho and Chremes contrast nicely, the one fiery and assertive, the other pusillanimous and tentative. Phormio's antics are possible in large measure because of the solid spadework of the slave Geta.

Legal Elements. In *Phormio* the law occupies much more of our attention than is usual in New Comedy. Certainly, there are many references to law and to court proceedings in Plautus and the extant plays and fragments of the Greeks. Threats of legal action or the flaunting of the bounds of law are especially common.[39] In this play, however, the legal maneuvering is an important structural element.

Geta tells us (124 ff.) that Antipho was afraid of the consequences if he married Phanium until Phormio concocted a clever scheme to make the law force him to do so: he brought suit on behalf of the girl under an Athenian statute requiring next of kin to marry an orphaned woman (or, as we are to learn later, to provide her with an adequate dowry). Antipho's part was to offer no defense so that he would be bound to be found liable by the court and so be "forced" to marry Phanium.

This legal maneuvering becomes a target for Demipho's anger, for it soon becomes clear that he is no stranger to the law. He is exasperated at his son's ineptitude:

DE: Will he say this to me, "I acted against my will. The law compelled me."? I'm listening; I grant it.

GE: (aside) You're saying the right things.

DE: But did the law compel him also in full awareness to give the case to his opponents without saying a word? (235–38)

Furthermore, Demipho knows the law well enough to ask why Antipho did not offer a dowry instead of marrying Phanium when judged liable (296–97). All in all, Demipho is a well-informed citizen of the sort one would expect to find in a society where men of affairs handled most their legal business personally.

More importantly, key segments of the play are constructed around "quasi-legal" wrangling. Phaedria's "defense" of his cousin causes his uncle Demipho to refer it as "pleading" and to say, "This one's in a jam, that one's on hand to defend his case" (266). The first meeting between Demipho and Phormio has a good deal of legal sparring, and the old man has brought three "legal advisors" with him to witness the meeting and offer their opinions (348 ff.). In their second meeting (898 ff.) the argument starts with threats of legal repercussions, until Phormio changes his tactics to blackmail.

Greek and Roman societies made law a much more personal matter than modern society with its professionals ready, even required in many cases, to represent the laity. These cultures were, therefore, quite sensitized to rhetoric, and so their drama exhibits rhetorical flare, whether it is in the adversarial conflicts of Greek tragedy, the glib manipulators of Aristophanes' stage, or the legal arguing of *Phormio.*[40]

Terence's *Phormio* and Apollodorus's *The Claimant.* All the plays of Terence have been subjected, as we have seen often, to scholarly scrutiny in an effort to ascertain as much as possible the nature of the Greek plays upon which they have been based. Such studies vary in their relevancy to a study of Terence per se, and we have referred to them rather little. In the case of *Phormio,* however, special mention of this question is in order.

On the one hand, there is a more or less general agreement that Terence stayed more than usually close to the play of Apollodorus; on the other, this piece is one of Terence's most successfully constructed so that we must be curious about the extent to which his own dramaturgical ability is at work as opposed to his skills as a translator. In fact, we are no better off with *Phormio* than with any other play of Terence with respect to our evidence for the nature of its model, though the general sparsity of Donatus's comments about direct Terentian modifications might be taken as tacit evidence for a close adherence to Apollodorus.

The careful study of *Phormio* from this perspective has, however, produced results that are very useful in focusing our attention on the care with which Terence worked. Sometimes we may think we are hearing Quintilian in phrases such as ". . . a daring stroke that would not have disgraced Menander himself,"[41] but a balanced study, such as that of Eckard Lefèvre, can be quite convincing in making the assertion that even when Terence follows the pattern of an Apollodoran scene, he changes the mood in such a way that it becomes his own material.[42] Thus, even where the constructive framework is little changed from that of another playwright, Terence makes the structure his own by subtle manipulation of elements of the individual scene.

Characters. The characters in *Phormio* are not drawn with the subtlety of Terence's best creations, but even in this play his exceptional ability to characterize is evident. Despite the fact that action dominates the play much more than characterization, Terence, especially through his use of contrasting pairs, presents an interesting cast. Furthermore, his major figures have aroused enough interest for there to be some range of opinion on them.

The Young Men: Phaedria and Antipho. Neither of the young men is a strong figure. Both must exhibit the kind of self-indulgence which we would expect from the situations into which they have entangled themselves. Their weaknesses are evident from their first appearance (152 ff.) where they vie with one another for the prize of being the more unfortunate and wretched. Antipho has his beloved Phanium at home but must face his father's anger; Phaedria has not become so desperately involved but must deal with a troublesome slave dealer to see his Pamphila.

Geta's entry, in the manner of the stock "running slave," brings the news of Demipho's return. Antipho is terrified, and, after trying his best to prepare himself for a meeting with his father, bolts the scene: "I certainly know myself and my shortcomings: I'm entrusting Phanium and my very life to you two" (217–18). Phaedria is left to represent his cousin to his outraged

uncle, but Antipho does not give up entirely. He returns full
of self-reproach for his cowardice (465 ff.) and is able to repay
Phaedria in part by helping him negotiate with the slave dealer
Dorio. He also takes the lead in urging Geta to find the 3,000
drachmas necessary to buy Pamphila before she is sold the next
day to a soldier.

Phaedria by comparison is the stronger figure. He keeps his
wits about him enough to face his uncle Demipho (231 ff.),
if not to get the better of the exchange. Demipho is not far
wrong in describing the relationship between the two young
men during his conversation with Phaedria:

> PH: But he's done nothing you should be angry at.
>
> DE: Well, see how everything's alike! They're just the same—
> know one, know them all.
>
> PH: Not at all!
>
> DE: This one's in a jam, that one's on hand to defend his case;
> when it's that one, this one's right on the spot. They have
> a mutual aid pact.
>
> GE: (aside) Know it or not, the old man's sketched out how
> these two act to a tee. (264–68)

Neither Phaedria nor Antipho is completely capable, however, and both rely on Geta and Phormio ultimately to help
them in their affairs. In the end they are what most of Terence's
young men are, indulged, a bit foolish, but not figures to whom
we are totally unsympathetic.

The Two Old Men: Demipho and Chremes. A far
greater contrast than the one between cousins is that between
the two brothers, Demipho and Chremes. Demipho is an active,
decisive figure, capable and knowledgeable, able to help his
brother Chremes, who is a much more passive individual. Perhaps the irony is intended that the stronger father should have
the weaker son and vice versa.

In his scenes with Phormio Demipho plays a worthy adver-
sary, for both know enough of the law to argue effectively in
legal terms.[43] On his return to the city he must contend both
with his son's foolish marriage and with his brother's family
problems, and he is kept busy. Even though he cannot unravel

everything, he is energetic to the end; it is Demipho who will not let Phormio blackmail Chremes (894 ff.) on grounds that a scoundrel like Phormio must not be allowed to prevail, and on the sound appraisal of the situation that matters have become too public to be kept from Nausistrata anyway.

Chremes is a more difficult figure. His bigamy is the source of a complex ethical problem, which affects our view of him fundamentally. Bigamy in the ancient world was surely not unprecedented, given slow communications between cities and relatively slow travel, all necessitating that some businessmen spent regular, long intervals in different cities. But there is no validation of such an arrangement in *Phormio*. When the facts are out, Demipho defends his brother to Nausistrata by explaining that his Lemnian family came about as the result of a drunken seduction. Chremes, upon learning that the girl was pregnant, cared for mother and child thenceforth, but did not live with the woman as a wife (1016 ff.). Thus, near the end of the play there is an attempt to put Chremes' actions in a better light: he is pictured as the victim of an unfortunate, human mistake, for which he took responsibility at considerable inconvenience. Such a description is consistent with the genuine concern Chremes has shown for his Lemnian family's welfare, but it glosses easily over his years of silence, and of trimming from his wife's rental moneys. We feel generally that Chremes' problems are the result of weakness rather than moral turpitude, and thus he must rely heavily on his brother when matters come to a head.

Phormio. Phormio's character is at once the finest accomplishment of the play and its most controversial element.[44] He is called *parasitus* by Geta (122), but he gives only the most perfunctory indications of the stock characteristics of the parasite (e.g., 331 ff. or 1052–53). For the most part he is characterized as a skillful rake with a lawyer's knowledge of the courts and an eagerness to take up a challenge. Although he is onstage only two times (315–440 and 829–1055; 351 lines total), his presence dominates the action throughout because so much is said about him and so much arises from his designs.

In fact, Phormio is perhaps best seen as having usurped the role of the "clever slave" (*servus callidus*). *Callidus* is applied to him directly by Geta: "I've seen no one cleverer (*callidiorem*) than Phormio" (591–92). Throughout the play the slave Geta exchanges roles with the parasite Phormio so that he becomes the faithful go-between, carrying out Phormio's plots; Phormio handles the planning and the delicate work of direct confrontation.

Despite his attractiveness as a character, Phormio has his less savory side. He is something of a sophist, or even a shyster, eager to make his will prevail on any point which interests him; moreover, he reverts to threats of blackmail when pressed and is pettily vengeful: "She'll have something to put in his ear as long as he lives" (1030), or "First of all, do you want to do something which will make you happy, Nausistrata, and slap your husband in the eye? . . . Invite me to dinner" (1053–54).

In summary, Phormio is the dominant role of the play, and perhaps the choice role in all of Terence, albeit he is no hero. He is the one example in Terentian comedy of a rogue controlling the stage, a circumstance not at all uncommon in the plays of Plautus.

Other Characters. Geta is a rather ordinary figure, even though he plays a large part in the play's action. The slave dealer Dorio eagerly describes himself as a prototype. Davus, the protactic character with whom Geta talks at the play's start, and Demipho's advisors are unremarkable. Chremes' wife, Nausistrata, is a rather richer figure.

Nausistrata could have become a typical shrewish wife. Her first words are a complaint about the way her husband has handled her affairs on Lemnos. When she learns about Chremes' double life, she is hurt and angry, nor does she forgive him readily. But Demipho is at pains to assure her that she has given him no cause to take another wife (1016), and her pique against Chremes is very reasonable. She exhibits finally a strength of character that compares well with her husband's pusillanimity, and she delivers one of the play's best lines: "Does it seem unworthy to you if your young son has one mistress, you with two wives?" (1040–41).

Theme. Unlike the other plays of Terence, there is not a clear-cut theme in *Phormio.* The play's action and characters dominate it in a way which overpowers potential thematic considerations. There are, however, three items worthy of comment.

We have seen that legal matters have a considerable part in the play's structure. One might suggest that this element comprises a satirical message on Roman legal maneuvering. The scoundrel Phormio can make the law work for him so that Demipho, a stalwart Roman gentleman of no mean legal ability, must resort in the last scene to physical violence to overcome him.[45] Yet, the legal bickering seems more of a dramatic means than a thematic end. It provides the arena in which Phormio's prepossessing personality can be displayed, but it does not develop a consistent philosophy about the law in the world of the play.

Another notable aspect of *Phormio* is the question of ethical behavior, especially in the actions of Phormio on behalf of the two young men, and of Chremes, in protecting his secret life. One might find in the play a triumph, at times ironically expressed, of moral action. Phormio, the rogue, abuses the law to produce a desirable effect, and one which is curiously legal when the story is finally told. Phaedria can liberate his Pamphila from an unpleasant slave dealer, whose character is not meant to inspire our sympathies. Chremes, who has deceived his wife, is forced finally to put himself at her mercy. But, whereas the play might have made much of this moral atmosphere, as in the case of the legal elements, this aspect is in the end only a part of the overall whole without compelling thematic significance.[46]

Finally, the events of *Phormio* happen in such a way that they become connected by the dictates of chance, and matters are resolved only by fortunate accident. The plays of New Comedy rely a great deal on luck to unravel their entwined problems, but even within this context *Phormio* is exceptional. In the Hellenistic world the concept of *tyche* (Latin: *fortuna*) gained a quite significant place. On one level Tyche became a personification and a deity; on another it was a subject for serious philosophical inquiry. Thus, it appears that the workings of Fortune were a fascination for the Hellenistic theatrical audience and became a theme of many New Comic plays. In Terence's play, however, this feature seems to be much more a legacy of the Hellenistic model. As *Phormio* progresses, we are not made to contemplate the fortuitous nature of human events; rather, we accept the coincidences as part of a conventional plot structure without any particular feeling of poignance.[47]

The Mother-in-Law (Hecyra)

Plot. The play begins with a conversation between Philotis, a young courtesan, and Syra, an old woman in the household of Bacchis, another courtesan with an establishment in the neighborhood. Syra is advising the young woman against being too soft toward her clients, while Philotis wonders if it is right to treat all men the same. They are met by Parmeno, family slave of Laches, his wife, Sostrata, and their son Pamphilus. Pamphilus was an ardent lover of Bacchis when Philotis left Athens two years before; she is surprised to hear he is now married and coaxes Parmeno to tell her what has happened.

The slave explains that Pamphilus came under heavy pressure from his father to marry. He resisted staunchly, but finally acceded to his father's wishes out of filial duty, and was promptly betrothed to Philumena, daughter of the neighbors, Phidippus and Myrrina. Just before the wedding he came to Parmeno in tears regretting his decision. Though he went through with the marriage, he resolved not to consort with his young wife and tried to continue his liaison with Bacchis. She grew cool toward him, however. He soon began to recognize the fine qualities of his wife who remained devoted to him despite his actions, and after a couple of months their marriage was consummated in mutual affection.

As Parmeno continues his story, however, we learn that trouble has arisen in the marriage: Pamphilus was sent to Imbros by his father to look after the estate of a deceased relative; in his absence some sort of problem arose between Philumena and her mother-in-law, Sostrata; the girl used the occasion of a religious festival to return to her parents' home and has neither come back to Sostrata, complaining now of illness, nor allowed her mother-in-law to visit her, although she has been very solicitous. That is where matters stand, as everyone awaits Pamphilus's return. Philotis leaves for a party at which she is expected, and Parmeno goes to the port to seek word of Pamphilus.

Laches and Sostrata come from their house in an argument. Laches, who spends most of his time at their country estate, has come into Athens because he has heard about the problems in his city household. He is berating Sostrata, accusing her of being a typical mother-in-law and of precipitating an argument with her daughter-in-law. Sostrata maintains her innocence and professes both concern for Philumena and confusion as to why the girl has taken a dislike to her.

At this moment Phidippus, Philumena's father, comes out of his house. The two old men greet each other cordially and express the hope that the problems can be resolved, but Phidippus is apprehensive for his daughter's welfare. They go off together to discuss the situation, leaving Sostrata pitifully lamenting the fact that mothers-in-law are typecast so badly.

After exiting, Parmeno returns from the port with Pamphilus, who has just arrived. Parmeno has been reporting the family problems to him, and Pamphilus is torn with confusion over his devotion to his wife and loyalty to his mother. As they near the houses, they hear Myrrina shout to her daughter, and Pamphilus rushes into his in-laws' house to find out what the problem is with his wife.

Sostrata returns, for she has heard that something has happened next door and is afraid Philumena's condition has worsened. As Parmeno tells her of Pamphilus's return, the latter himself comes out. He tells his mother that Philumena is better; she returns to her house, relieved. He then sends Parmeno to the port for his baggage. After the slave leaves, he muses about what he has discovered inside: Philumena is in childbirth. Myrrina had rushed to meet him to explain the pregnancy, for they have been married only nine months, and the marriage went unconsummated for two months. Shortly before their marriage, however, Philumena was raped by an unknown assailant. She begged Pamphilus not to reveal the details of their first months of marriage. If their early marital problems somehow do become known, she plans to claim that the child is premature. At any rate, she promised to destroy the infant immediately. Pamphilus is crushed by the development. He loves Philumena, but he cannot accept the new situation.

Parmeno returns with another slave, Sosia, bringing the baggage. Pamphilus realizes that he knows about the delay in the marriage's consummation, so he sends him away to the acropolis on pretext of keeping an appointment with a fictitious friend, thereby removing him from the scene of the birth.

The old men, Laches and Phidippus, return eager to find

Pamphilus, of whose arrival they have learned. Pamphilus is too confused to deal with them, however, so he merely reports that Philumena seems irreconcilable toward her mother-in-law, and he suggests a divorce. The old men are not willing to accept such a solution, since they feel that the difficulties between the women should be resolved rather than the marriage ended, so they go off to confront their womenfolk.

Soon after, Myrrina rushes from her house excitedly talking about Phidippus's discovering the baby. He follows her full of anger that the pregnancy had been kept secret and orders that the baby not be harmed. He blames the marital problems on Myrrina, whom he accuses of a mother-in-law's jealousies, and goes off to attend the care of the child, leaving her onstage to lament her situation. Before she goes in, she elaborates on the rape of Philumena, mentioning that her attacker pulled a ring from her finger.

Sostrata and Pamphilus return. Sostrata has decided for the sake of her son's marriage to abandon the house in Athens and join her husband in the country. Pamphilus protests, but Laches, who has been listening from the doorway, is pleased with the idea. He sends his wife to pack. He and Pamphilus are met by Phidippus, full of news. Laches learns for the first time about the child, and Phidippus asserts his belief that Myrrina, not Sostrata, has been the instigator of Philumena's behavior. Pamphilus does not accept this information as a basis for reconciliation, of course, and the two old men are frustrated at his reaction. Laches suddenly decides that his obstinacy must be a means to destroy his marriage so that he can return to Bacchis. Without replying to the charge, Pamphilus bolts off in confusion, and the two old men decide to call in Bacchis in order to clear up the matter.

Laches returns with her, and she assures him that since the marriage she had discontinued her affair with his son. He convinces her, against her sense of social decorum, to go inside and tell this to the women.

Parmeno returns from his errand, disgusted that Pamphilus's "friend" never appeared. Bacchis comes from the house and eagerly greets him. She sends him to look for Pamphilus with the message, which she says he will understand, that the ring he gave her belongs to Philumena. While she waits for their return, she reports what transpired within: her ring was recognized as the one taken from Philumena by her assailant; but Pamphilus had given her the ring one evening, arriving unexpected and drunk, with the story, produced after some prodding, that he had just attacked a young woman in the street; thus, Pamphilus is the child's father after all.

Parmeno returns with Pamphilus. The master is overjoyed at the turn of events; Parmeno does not understand what is happening, and it is clear that Pamphilus has not confided in him about the rape. They resolve not to tell the fathers, but let them merely assume that the young couple is reconciled as they wished. And so the play ends happily.

The plot of *The Mother-in-Law* is the slowest of all Terence's plays. Furthermore, it contains several details which might be considered contradictory or confusing. For example, how long after the rape were Pamphilus and Philumena married? We know that the marriage was not consummated until two months after the wedding and that we are in the "seventh month" after Philumena "came to" Pamphilus (cf. 393–94). Does this mean that Philumena came to her wedding fully aware she was pregnant? Or, does "came to" mean her coming to Pamphilus's bed, two months after her wedding and only a little more since the rape? Thus, has Pamphilus been the victim of deception throughout, or did Philumena come to her wedding innocent of any knowledge of her pregnancy, only to be driven to desperate action when she was faced with her prospering womb? We may infer the latter, but the point remains vexed.[48] Also, we might question the discrepancy between Parmeno's report that Pamphilus visited Bacchis frequently after his marriage until her rapacity cooled his ardor (157 ff.) with her oath to Laches that she broke with him immediately after his marriage (750–52). Here the difficulty is imaginary, for it is part of Parmeno's characterization that he assumes more than he knows, but there remains the possibility of confusing the audience. On the whole, however, the plot moves smoothly and is cleverly constructed, despite the fact that to grasp its subtleties requires extraordinary attention from the audience.

Still, this is Terence's most unusual play, and we cannot fail to note its problems in production. Critics have often cited its unusual plot as the reason: Roman audiences were not ready for something both slow-moving and complicated. It does have its supporters, however, and we should recall that it is by no means certain to what extent problems with production were due to audience disfavor or to the sabotage of Terence's literary rivals.

Structure.   As in other respects, so in construction, *The Mother-in-Law* differs from Terence's other plays. Most notably, it does not employ the "duality" method so favored in other pieces. Rather, our attention is focused on one problem alone and on one young man. Of greater significance, the play often teeters, until near its conclusion, on the edge of becoming romantic tragedy rather than New Comedy. Its seriousness of spirit is remarkable. And yet it is assuredly a comedy. Its serious mood is alleviated in part by the careful use of characters in traditionally comic situations interspersed through the play.

The "Prologue Problem."   We have seen how Terence eschewed the use of an expository prologue in all his plays, using the portion of the play usually reserved for the prologue to make statements about his dramatic methods and the criticisms of his enemies (cf. the discussion in chap. 2). Thus his plays do not rely on audience omniscience but unfold before an audience "in suspense." The opening scenes, therefore, bear especial burden for exposition.

In his other plays the plots are based on such stock situations that the eventual resolutions are obvious enough to the informed play-goer, and the "suspense" lies more in the handling of specifics than in any surprise. *The Mother-in-Law,* however, has an unusual story, and although it employs a stock resolution, the information necessary to recognize it is withheld until late in the play. The effect is radical, especially in view of what we know about the practices of Greek authors. Therefore, critics have examined Terence's structure by speculating on the changes he has made in his model by Apollodorus of Carystus. Principally, they posit that the Greek play contained a prologue, perhaps following the conversation between Philotis and Parmeno. This prologue would have corrected and expanded upon the information just provided by the slave.[49]

Were there a prologue, we would, in fact, be able to evaluate

Parmeno's information early on, instead of being surprised later by contradictory revelations; we would be better informed about the relationship between the rape and the wedding; we would know in advance the reason for Philumena's leaving Sostrata; and we would know what sort of resolution to expect. In Terence's play, whether or not his original had a prologue, the exposition leads to a different state of audience awareness. The tension created by the characters' interactions is not lessened by an underlying surety of how the happy ending will be achieved. We must instead go with the play as it unfolds and change with it as it changes, evaluating events on the information at hand until rather late in the play.[50]

The Protatic Character Philotis. The opening scenes, as we have noted, are quite important to Terence for providing expository information. The use of protatic characters is common as a means of stimulating a dialogue between a principal character and a figure who will command no more of our attention. In *The Mother-in-Law* Terence uses such a scene especially well.

The first characters on stage are Philotis, the young courtesan, and Syra, an old woman in the house of Bacchis. They are discussing the correct attitude of a courtesan toward her clients. Syra argues that every man must be fleeced, and rightly so, for they are all interested only in pleasure gained as cheaply as possible. Philotis thinks this a harsh position: "Should I think no man different?" (66); "But surely it's not right to be the same to everybody" (71).

Their conversation is an example of the technique Terence uses to establish his comic mood. This is a stock situation in which an old woman preaches her jaded philosophy to a more idealistic young woman (another example is found in Plautus's *The Haunted House* [157 ff.], where a courtesan, Philematium, is instructed in the ways of the world by her old maid, Scapha, as she is grooming). Thus Terence begins a rather unconventional play with a quite conventional scene. As we will see, he uses conventional comic motifs at intervals in order to keep the mood from becoming too somber. In addition, Philotis's responses allude, here at the beginning of the play, to its principal theme. Throughout, *The Mother-in-Law* presents the effects of typecasting, just the practice which Philotis is questioning.

The Use of Parmeno. In a play that features sharp conflicts between major figures to such an extent that human sadness seems a likely outcome, Parmeno is just the sort of figure whose presence provides contact with the ordinary comic world.

In the first part of the play we have every reason to expect that the slave will be Pamphilus's advisor and confidant. In his conversation with Philotis he gives the impression that Pamphilus turns to him in need regularly (cf. 130–34), and he talks like an advisor when they enter together from the port at our first view of Pamphilus (281 ff.). But, when Pamphilus learns of the true situation with Philumena, he is eager to get Parmeno out of the way, a bit embarrassed that the slave knows too much about his early months of marriage (409–14). Thus, if we had thought that Parmeno would be the "clever slave" who would resolve his master's problems, we are surprised.[51]

Parmeno enters (415) in conversation with a fellow slave who has been abroad with Pamphilus. Their conversation, like that between Philotis and Syra, is part of the conventional repertoire of slave scenes, as they complain about their tasks. He meets Pamphilus and is sent off immediately to await a fictitious friend of his master in another part of the city, a "wild goose" chase which was a popular motif of New Comedy.

Parmeno returns (799) just in time to meet Bacchis and deliver the message about the ring to Pamphilus, with whom he soon comes back. He is completely in the dark as to why they are so happy at the discovery of the ring, and so we know that despite Parmeno's self-importance his master has not regularly confided in him at all. In response to Pamphilus's profuse expressions of gratitude he can only say, "I've done more good today without knowing why than I've ever done before when I've tried!" (880). With this line the play ends.

Thus Terence has used Parmeno to provide a conventional comic focus at key points in his play in order to relieve the more serious moments with stock antics. He surprises us in so doing by showing us a slave different from the sort Parmeno had led us to believe he was, and he brings his play to a thoroughly joyous conclusion, which Parmeno's confusion underscores.

Characters.   As we have said so often, Terence has been praised by critics of many eras for his skill in characterization.

The Mother-in-Law is his most radical experiment in character. Depth of characterization in New Comedy does not arise from unique creations. In a theater where the stock types are well understood by the audience, however, effective portrayals can be derived from subtle deviations from the norm. In *The Mother-in-Law* we find stock figures common to New Comedy, but they are drawn in an unusual way and interact differently than in most plays of the genre.

Donatus recognized that the play had novel qualities in his commentary.[52] And yet, the richness of the characters may be regarded as more of a liability than an asset, for many have felt that their unusualness, combined with the play's slow pace, yields a dramatic whole which is less satisfactory than Terence's other pieces. It is often suggested that this failing can be cited as the reason behind the problems in production.[53] Much of this sort of criticism is based on taste, though it would be hard on any grounds to rate *The Mother-in-Law* as Terence's best play. Certainly it was not his most popular in antiquity. Yet, a modern audience looking back on New Comedy from a dramatic perspective schooled to accept comedies of quite varied sorts, may well find this play a refreshing variant of a somewhat repetitive tradition.

The Men: Laches, Phidippus, Pamphilus. It is unusual to have a play without an unmarried young man. That is, however, our situation in *The Mother-in-Law*. If one reads the play with a mind too saturated with the stock plots of New Comedy, it is easy to fall unawares into the error of reacting to Pamphilus as the comic young man in love, but, of course, he is a married man, and so has a quite different status in the Roman world. Nor do we find the expected "blocking figure," a father bent on keeping him from his beloved. Instead, Laches works very hard to bring his son and Philumena together. But, as we will see, the characters also exhibit stock traits.

It comes perhaps as a surprise to be reminded by Donatus that Laches is the play's principal character, based on the number of lines assigned to him, to be sure. Pamphilus is second in "volume," Phidippus third.

Laches enters (198) in a stock argument with his wife, Sostrata. He blames her for causing trouble with her daughter-in-law, assuming that she is acting like a typical mother-in-law, for whom no one is good enough for her son. Phidippus's first words (243–45) are to assure his daughter Philumena that he is concerned about her feelings. Such concern for the son's interests on the one hand, the daughter's on the other, is reminiscent of the situation in *The Girl from Andros*. And Phidippus is just as willing as Laches to indict his wife as the malefactor when he learns of the birth of the child (cf. 536 ff.). Laches plays the role of the irascible father well enough when he decides that Pamphilus is being perverse in order to break up his marriage and return to Bacchis (cf. 671 ff.), and he assumes the position of the father working against a profligate son.

But, despite these affinities with stock characters, the situation is such that the old men's actions are not quite those of strictly conventional figures. Laches is driven throughout by concern. His relationship with Sostrata is not terrible, as we see from his general willingness to take her with him to the country when she decides to leave the young people alone. And his efforts are in fact directed not toward depriving Pamphilus of pleasure but toward enhancing his chances for happiness. Phidippus, much like Chremes in *The Girl from Andros,* remains committed to his daughter's happiness, and so any disagreeableness in his character is ameliorated.

Pamphilus acts the part of the young lover with his indecision and confusion. But these traits in him are moving rather than humorous. Based on all that he knows of the situation, he has found himself in dire straits: his mother accused falsely; the young wife, whom he has grown to love, the mother, seemingly, of a child sired by another; and he himself thrust into a quandary between love and duty.

His is an ironic position. Whereas other plays tend to show fathers eager to take their sons away from unacceptable love affairs by binding them to an acceptable marriage, here Pamphilus is on the other side of the process. He has been led away from Bacchis to a successful marriage. But, instead of the happy result one would expect, Pamphilus finds himself in an unhappy situation indeed. His "off-center" position makes his character quite effective. The adolescent confusion is comic in the young lover, but in the young husband it is touching. The young man is all the more contrasted with the old men who are considerably more jaded in their marital relationships.

The Women: Sostrata, Myrrina, Bacchis. Norwood has said of *The Mother-in-Law,* "It is a woman's play—not feminist, not expounding any special doctrine, but with women as the chief sufferers, the chief actors, the bearers here of the Terentian *humanitas.* "[54] Thais, of *The Eunuch,* may be Terence's strongest female figure, but surely *The Mother-in-Law* does, in fact, bring women to the forefront of the play's theme in a way not approximated elsewhere.

Neither of the wives in other plays, Sostrata in *The Self-Tormentor* and Nausistrata in *Phormio,* is given the depth of character of the women here. Certainly the other Sostrata and Nausistrata are significant roles, each a notch above the colorless ciphers or the henpecks often found in Plautus, but in *The Mother-in-Law,* especially with the role of Sostrata, we find characters who demand real sympathy.

Terence is careful to give us a positive view of Sostrata from the start, when Parmeno tells Philotis of her efforts to accommodate her daughter-in-law and to bring her home. We are prepared then to be sympathetic to her attempts to acquit herself to Laches when we first see her. Her only negative trait, at least as concerns a conservative Roman audience, is her tendency to prefer the luxury of the city and the company of her friends to Laches' rustic life. But her relationship with Pamphilus is excellent, as attested by his devotion to her. She is, in fact, the victim of stereotyping on Laches' part, and her short monologue (274–80) both establishes this point clearly and expresses well the extent to which she has suffered over the situation.

Unlike the case of other wives, her characterization does not stop with her encounter with Laches. Sostrata's relationship with her son is seen firsthand (336 ff.). Furthermore, the depth of her commitment is shown us when she comes out personally to tell him of her decision to forego the city so that the way will be cleared for Philumena's return:

This is now my major concern, that my long life not be a burden to anyone and that no one wait eagerly for my death. (595–96)

She asks of Pamphilus, "Allow me, please, to escape the bad repute people hear of women" (600).

Myrrina is drawn in less depth, but she too is hurt by the

stereotyping of women. Our first view of her is from Pamphilus's description of her efforts to protect Philumena's reputation (378 ff.). Her desperation comes through clearly from his report. Thus, as when Laches accused Sostrata, so when Phidippus attacks her for keeping the birth of the child secret, we are prepared to take her side. Her comment aside when he accuses her of trying to undermine the marriage because she had disapproved of Pamphilus's relationship with Bacchis, "I'd rather he suspect any reason than the real one" (540), is indicative of her willingness to shield Philumena by bearing the brunt of accusations herself.

Bacchis stands in obvious contrast to the two matrons, but in an important sense she must be compared with them. Just as Sostrata wants to do the best for Pamphilus, so Bacchis is eager also to help him. And like the two older women she is the object of typecasting (cf. 774–76).[55] But, when Laches suggests that she tell her story directly to the women, she is appropriately concerned that her presence before married women will be an embarrassment. She, like Sostrata, has a monologue (816–40) that does much to express her character. Her distinctiveness is underscored by these lines:

I'm glad so much happiness has come his [Pamphilus's] way because of me, even if other courtesans don't feel like this. It's not in our professional interest for a lover to be happy in his marriage. (833–35)

Theme. We have seen a number of examples of the unusual qualities found in *The Mother-in-Law.* The play is also exceptional in the seriousness of its theme. Terence's plays generally have a coherent message, but never expressed in the severe tone which is assumed for most of this play. Seriousness of theme does not provide automatic access to dramatic success, as the number of critics of this piece will attest, and it may be that the play is more successfully studied than played. The two issues it raises, however, the effects of stereotyping and the position of women, deserve our examination.

Unfair Stereotyping. The plot of *The Mother-in-Law* is constructed throughout on wrong conclusions. Its action is put into motion by Philumena's deceptions which lead to unfair blame on Sostrata. Laches' actions stem first from an unfair assumption that mothers-in-law in general and Sostrata in particular relish the discomfort of their daughters-in-law; he then moves to a wrong conclusion about Pamphilus's motives, based on the notion that young men are overcommitted to their love affairs. Phidippus is no better in that he jumps to the wrong conclusion as to why the baby's existence has been kept secret, accusing Myrrina unjustly and further complicating things.

The effects of this tendency to stereotype go deeper than the level of mere plot. Speeches by various characters show that it is a key issue in the play. Philotis puts it forth at the play's beginning when she disagrees with old Syra that all lover's should be treated alike. Sostrata's concern for Philumena is carefully outlined in Parmeno's description of events before the opening of the play. Thus, we can see the unfairness of typecasting clearly when Laches says in his anger:

So all mothers-in-law and daughters-in-law dislike each other. They're equally ready to fight their husbands; their stubbornness is just alike. I think they all go to the same school for meanness, and if there is a school, I know for sure she's its principal. (201–4)

In her monologue Sostrata cries, "Oh God, we're all hateful to our husbands in the same unjust way because of a few women who act so as to make us all seem to deserve disgrace" (274–75). Finally, Laches quickly typecasts Pamphilus as the unrepentant lover, and Phidippus warns against believing Bacchis, simply because she is a courtesan.

As much as the women suffer from this unfair treatment, it is Pamphilus who illustrates its greatest harm. He is caught squarely between his heart and his sense of duty (cf. 403–8), certainly because of the extraordinary ironies of the plot, but also because he cannot cope with two typical responses. He cannot accept the bastard readily as his son or find a way to forgive Philumena for the situation despite her innocence of intentional wrongdoing, and he feels drawn to his mother against his wife out of filial duty.

In this atmosphere an important irony emerges. Whereas in a less charged setting the fact that Pamphilus is after all the father of the child would be simply an element of the stock plot, here it emphasizes the harm in his making wrong assumptions in the same way as have the older men. He is very much in danger of treating his wife with the same unfairness with which they have treated theirs. Thus, one of the important triumphs of the play's comic spirit is that the young marriage retains more hope than the old ones. The young couple can rise above the behavior of their elders, though, in keeping with the play's mixed tone, it has been a near thing.

The Position of Women. We must avoid the urge to make modern social criticism of *The Mother-in-Law*. In any terms, however, the female characters bear the brunt of the males' ill-conceived accusations. We have seen how the women, Philotis, Sostrata, Bacchis, question the fairness of stereotypical reactions. But they are all, including Myrrina, the victims of this attitude. The slave Parmeno expresses the general attitude well when he is trying to assure Pamphilus that all will be well with his mother and Philumena:

How is it that little boys get mad over little problems? Why, they have weak self-control. These women are about the same as little boys with their flighty minds. (310–12)

Coming from a character such as Parmeno, the gratuitous comparison is especially acrid.

One of the most satisfying outcomes of the play is, as we have just seen, that Pamphilus and Philumena overcome their difficulties. The young man has not resorted to the bickering common to the stock relationship of older couples, but it seems that he too is destined for an unhappy marriage. After his situation is unexpectedly resolved, Pamphilus gives us reason to think about this proposition when he says, alluding to his desire not to tell the old men the details of his reconciliation with Philumena, "I'd rather it not happen in the same way as in the comedies where everybody knows everything" (866–67). The resolution of *The Mother-in-Law*, like so much else in the play, is not in the usual New Comic manner.

The Brothers (Adelphoe)

Plot. Micio begins the play with a monologue in which he expresses concern that his son Aeschinus has not returned home from his evening's entertainment. He compares his approach to handling his son with that of his brother Demea toward his son Ctesipho. Both children were born to Demea, but Micio, a bachelor, adopted the older, Aeschinus. He has dealt with Aeschinus tolerantly, while Demea holds a tighter rein. Micio has lived a relatively easygoing life in Athens; Demea a more austere existence in the country.

Demea enters, excited about reports that Aeschinus has broken into someone's house and taken away a slave girl. The two brothers have words. Micio implies that Demea is too involved in the raising of the son he has given for adoption; Demea is frustrated at Micio's casual attitude toward Aeschinus's behavior. They calm themselves, but Demea exits, still hurt. Micio confesses that he too has been concerned over Aeschinus's behavior, though he would only fan Demea's flame to admit as much openly. He had recently thought Aeschinus might be quieting down and thinking of marriage, and so he is all the more concerned at the present turn of events.

He leaves to find his son, who enters on his heels, bringing the slave girl with him. Sannio, the slave dealer from whose establishment she has been taken, is following. Aeschinus instructs a slave to restrain him physically. The two argue over Aeschinus's high-handed actions; the young man offers to pay the cost of the girl, without giving Sannio any profit, and goes inside his house. Sannio is left to fume until Syrus, Micio's slave and a confidant of Aeschinus and Ctesipho, comes out to talk with him. He convinces Sannio to accept Aeschinus's offer, knowing that the slave dealer is eager to leave town on a business trip.

Ctesipho enters, and we learn that the slave girl is his mistress. Aeschinus has become involved in order to help his younger brother against the slave dealer. Ctesipho is awed by his older brother's decisive action and terrified that his father may find out about his affair. Aeschinus and Syrus return to go with Sannio and pay for the slave girl. Aeschinus and his brother talk, and we learn that Ctesipho had become desperate over his problems, finally telling Aeschinus, who came immediately to his rescue. The younger brother is sent inside to comfort his mistress, and Aeschinus, Syrus, and Sannio go off to finish their business.

Two women, Sostrata and her old maid Canthara, come from their house, excitedly talking of going for a midwife and of looking for Aeschinus. It becomes clear that he is the father of the child which is about to be born and has been the women's patron for some time. They are met by the slave Geta, who enters in the manner of a "running slave" to deliver the news that Aeschinus has deserted them. The slave has learned about the abduction of the slave girl and has leapt to the obvious conclusion. Sostrata resolves to seek the help of a relative, Hegio.

Demea returns upset because he has heard that Ctesipho was involved in seizing the slave girl. At this same moment Syrus comes in talking about Micio's help in paying off the slave dealer. Demea is disgusted to hear that his brother is an abettor in the affair, and Syrus plays to him by comparing his conduct favorably to that of Micio. He also tells him that Ctesipho was present at the fracas only in order to try to stop Aeschinus. Demea is eager to find his son, and Syrus tries to get him out of the way by telling him that Ctesipho has returned to the country. Before the old man leaves, he is met by Hegio and learns about Aeschinus's relationship with young Pamphila, Sostrata's daughter and the girl who has just given birth. Since Hegio believes that Aeschinus has deserted her in favor of the slave girl, he is eager to make Demea aware of the problem. The old man is all the more excited, and now decides to go off to find Micio. Hegio goes inside, but returns shortly to look for Micio also.

Ctesipho and Syrus enter, and Ctesipho expresses his concern that Demea, not finding him in the country, will come back to look for him. Syrus promises to deal with his father, simply by praising Ctesipho to him. Demea returns suddenly, not having found Micio but having learned that Ctesipho did not go to the country. Syrus meets the old man and delights him with a fictitious account of Ctesipho's efforts to block Aeschinus from taking the slave girl. Demea's eagerness to find Ctesipho gives the slave the opportunity to send him off on a complicated "wild goose chase" to a made-up location where Ctesipho is supposed to have gone to have some furniture repaired.

Micio and Hegio enter, and it is clear that Hegio has informed Micio of the situation with Pamphila. Micio has accepted responsibility. As the two go into Sostrata's house, Aeschinus comes onstage distraught at having learned that he is thought to have abandoned Pamphila. Micio comes out, sees his son, and resolves to test him by pretending to be a bystander at events transpiring inside, where the family has decided that Pamphila must marry a relative to relieve her present condition. Aeschinus's façade collapses, and Micio, pleased to be assured of Aeschinus' moral worth, remonstrates with him for not seeking help sooner. Aeschinus is overjoyed at his father's support and his permission to marry Pamphila.

Demea now returns from his futile search for Ctesipho and encounters Micio as his brother is coming out of Sostrata's house. The two again argue. Demea is frustrated to find Micio calm in the face of the tangled state of Aeschinus's affairs; Micio leaves his brother with the argument unresolved to return to help with the wedding plans. Syrus comes out of Micio's house at this point shouting over his shoulder to a fellow slave a message for Ctesipho, and Demea suddenly discovers that his son is with the slave girl. He rushes in to find out what is happening, and Syrus beats a retreat.

The two old men meet again in front of the houses a bit later and yet another argument begins. Demea is beside himself over the way the two boys have behaved and have been allowed to behave. Micio tries to assuage his anger and to show him that their own conduct when they were young was controlled by poverty, not by disinclination to do the things their sons have been doing. He finally convinces his brother to join the celebration within.

Demea returns after a while to deliver a curious speech: he has seen how eagerly both young men come to his brother and shun him and concludes that his efforts to build character by holding a tight rein have led only to his being disliked; he resolves to make a volte-face and achieve some of his brother's popularity.

There follows a series of events in which Demea incites Aeschinus to make excessive requests. He supports him in his impatience at the slowness of the wedding plans and advises him to ignore the ceremonies by simply boring a hole in the garden wall and bringing his bride home. When Micio comes out to protest, Demea tells him it is what Aeschinus wants, and Micio's acquiescence is an opening for Demea to force even more outrages on him. He enlists Aeschinus to help him convince Micio to marry Pamphila's mother, Sostrata, to free both Syrus and his slave wife, and finally to give Hegio a small farm which he owns. After forcing his brother into this display of doting on his son's opinion, Demea reveals that he has done it all to show Micio's shortcomings. He assures Aeschinus of his own love and offers in the future to act as advisor to the two young men when they feel the need for a restraining hand. Aeschinus agrees, but begs that Ctesipho be allowed to keep the slave girl. Demea agrees to this last concession, ending the play.

The Brothers is generally considered Terence's finest piece. Certainly, it has been his most studied. If one accepts the traditional dating of the play as his last, then its exceptionally fine plot management can be cited as an example of his developed skills. On the other hand, the dating of the plays has been open to serious debate, and there are some features of the plot of *The Brothers* which have given even its supporters pause.

The crux of this problem is Demea's change after line 854. It is not simply a question of characterization, that is, to what extent are his perceptions genuinely modified, or his actions simply a ruse to defend his position at last. Rather, we must ask whether the topsy-turvy ending affects radically the understanding of the play's message that has been built up through the first four-fifths of the plot. Moreover, is this sudden change effective, or is it a weakness, a sort of *deus ex machina* that is not worthy of the rest of the play's structure? Analysis of this problem will occupy us soon.

The scholarship devoted to this play over the past century has produced many sensitive studies. Some, in the tradition of source studies which we have seen in the case of all Terence's plays, have examined Terence's *The Brothers* in relation to its Greek models, spurred on especially by the information from the play's prologue that a scene from a play by Diphilus was incorporated into the framework provided by the principal model from Menander. Others have concentrated solely on Terence's play itself. In either case scholarly activity has been heavy in comparison with the interest in the other five plays, and one can find support from carefully reasoned studies for a variety of opinions concerning every important feature of the play. Fore-warned that the state of disagreement is especially chaotic for a reading of *The Brothers,* we can move to our analyses of its structure, characters, and theme.[56]

Structure.   In structure *The Brothers* exhibits those charac-teristics one might easily predict from a reading of Terence's other plays. It utilizes the "duality" method fully and has a well-paced mixture of comic moods which assures that serious content will be interspersed with broad, farcical humor.

"Duality" Construction.   The affairs of the two young brothers are of the types found in other double plots. Aeschinus is involved with a girl who may be a marriage partner, albeit she is dowerless; Ctesipho is interested in a slave girl with whom marriage is not a question. Aeschinus' affair is by far the more serious matter, but the resolution of his problems comes about, ironically, because of his efforts to help his brother secure his slave girl.

The older brothers too have their "duality subplots." The relationship of each to his son is well developed, and these relationships are part of the larger issue, which draws clear lines between the brothers, concerning the best approach to handling adolescent children. That question comprises the theme of the play, so that we are very interested in which brother proves to be the better theorist. In the end their relationships to each other and to their children become even more entwined than the love affairs of the two young men.

Even more effective than the use of duality in the plot line is the advantage taken of the pairs of characters. The play's title has an obvious double meaning. Both the young men and their fathers are brothers. There are two sets of natural pairs, then, easily compared one with the other. But Terence goes further. Another comparison develops from the juxtaposition of the relationship between Micio and Aeschinus to that of Demea and Ctesipho. Thus, the play utilizes a number of inter-locking comparisons made possible by its dualities.

All the plays save *The Mother-in-Law* use duality in some form, though only vestigial use is made in *The Girl from Andros.* The complexity and effectiveness achieved by the use of this struc-tural device in *The Brothers* are quite exceptional, however, even by Terentian standards. This fact may be the single strongest argument to support the traditional place of the play as Terence's last production.

Farcical Elements. Although the theme of *The Brothers* is as serious as any in Terence, the play itself retains a thoroughly humorous tone throughout. Terence was at pains to insure that there are broad farcical elements everywhere.

The most obvious example of broad humor is the sequence based on a scene from Diphilus (cf. 6–10), involving the slave dealer Sannio (155 ff.). Not only is Sannio a prototypical stock character (cf. his own words at 160–61), but Aeschinus treats him outrageously, occasioning much visual humor and ample physical abuse. Terence went out of his way to bring this material into his play, in order, we must assume, to make the plot he found in Menander more sprightly.

This fondness for the broader rather than more subdued comic touch can be seen in Micio's confrontation with his son Aeschinus after the old man has learned about the situation with Pamphila. Micio has prided himself on trying to keep open the routes of communication with his son, and yet Aeschinus has withheld this important part of his life from his father. We might well expect a serious conversation when the two meet. Instead, Micio decides to toy with his son and to tease an admission from him. He learns early in their meeting that Aeschinus is morally responsible. "He's blushed. Everything's fine" (643). After that, he plays on his fears to our amusement.

Demea's role is also important for keeping the tone of the play upbeat. Although his position is consistently that of the sober, sensible conservative, his manner is excessive and comical. He can be frustrated by his brother into extravagant ranting, and he becomes the target of the slave Syrus's outlandish parody of his self-satisfied manner (419–32). Finally, after his radical change, he goes about doing things that make the play's final sequence broadly farcical.

Demea's Change of Heart. In a play that exhibits so tight a structure it is especially disconcerting to find a perplexing change of direction when the plot is 90 percent completed. At line 855 Demea comes out of Micio's house, where he has been celebrating Aeschinus's marriage, to announce that he now sees how his brother's approach to the children has brought him their affection while his own has gained their resentment.

He resolves to change his ways in order to gain the advantages of a reputation for permissiveness. He proceeds to dominate the rest of the play and to force Micio into more and more absurd concessions in catering to Aeschinus.

Our understanding of this action has fundamental implications for interpreting the play as a whole. Is it a rather clumsy ending attached to a skillfully constructed play to modify our feelings that severity is an unsuccessful approach to childrearing and to leave us instead with a sort of Aristotelian mean? Is it simply another example of the play's farcical humor not to be overrated as an indication of a new thematic statement? Is it a clever device for providing the comedy with a surprise ending meant to overturn our conviction that Micio's theories are correct by showing that they actually lead to absurd doting?

There is no clear-cut answer to these questions. As we have indicated would be the case, there is wide disagreement as to how this ending should be evaluated. In such situations, where qualified interpreters are so divided, it usually rests with the director to establish a "meaning" for the play. It is clear that *The Brothers* may be directed along several lines. We need not be left, however, without an opinion as to which course to take.

In light of the play's tendency to use broad humor, while it treats at the same time a serious theme, we should not be too surprised at the turn of events near its end. Terence makes it clear that Demea is enjoying his fling at openhandedness (cf. 884–85, 895–96, 911–15) and that he is intentionally trying to force Micio's hand (958). With hindsight we might suggest that the ending is just what one would wish, a "serious farce." Demea has been the butt of the play's jokes thus far; now it is Micio's turn. Neither of the old men has been depicted as perfect up to now; both have shown strengths and weaknesses. Demea's weaknesses have generally been on display, but now it is time for Micio to confront his own. Thus, the view, and it is the traditional one, that the play finally suggests a mean in childraising somewhere between Demea's sternness and Micio's leniency, is quite in keeping with what we might expect from the structure as a whole.

Characters. There are several well-drawn characters in *The Brothers,* more, in fact, than in any other of Terence's plays.

It is very much a play of character, despite its farcical elements. Terence plays off his characters one against the other with great skill so that Micio, Demea, Aeschinus, and Ctesipho all come alive through what is said both by them and about them. Of the other characters, Syrus, Hegio, and Sannio all deserve some mention.

The "duality" composition, as we have seen, invites comparison between the major figures. There are, in fact, several ways of aligning the pairs. One combination, which is quite useful in considering the play's theme, is to place together sons and fathers. In this way we can gain some understanding of how good a relationship each has achieved through his theory of handling children.

Micio and Aeschinus. Many would consider Micio the strongest character in all of Terence. He moves through the play confidently, taking the upper hand in all his encounters and acting always the gentleman until the play's final segment. It is easy to accentuate the positive qualities of his character, but we must be careful to note that Terence does not portray him without faults.

Micio occupies our attention for a considerable length of time at the play's beginning, first with his monologue (26–80), then in his conversation with Demea (80–140), and finally in his short monologue, which sums up the situation (141–54). As usual, the section bears the burden of both characterization and setting of scene. We learn about the disagreement between the two brothers on the question of childraising. We are also given a good look at Micio and Demea in action. It is important to remember, however, that much of our information is slanted to Micio's point of view, because he provides us with background information, and he controls the conversation with Demea.

This initial segment does reveal the essential outlines of Micio's character and his philosophy. He is committed to his son and outspoken on his ideas about how best to handle his upbringing. He prefers to picture himself as liberal in direct opposition to his brother, whom he paints as conservative. He is free with his money and hopes that by encouraging and supporting his son in a range of experiences he will foster in him independence, openness, and good rapport with his father. Only in this way, he contends, can the child's true character come through, else children will learn to dissimulate before their parents and be themselves when alone. Micio is at great pains to oppose his ideas to those of his brother, to such an extent that we must feel that this is an old debate and one in which he is eager to curry favor for his side.

This basic character holds true in the other situations involving Micio. He is decisive in dealing with the slave dealer (364 ff.), eager to meet the commitment with which Hegio presents him, and willing to admonish his son while at the same time supporting him (635 ff.).

As a counterconsideration to these positive traits, however, we should observe some other characteristics that Terence is careful to develop as well. Notably, Micio does not treat his brother Demea with complete candor or fairness. He justifies himself by saying that Demea's disposition is such that any attempt to agree with him only abets his intolerance (141–47). Even so, he goes out of his way to stand exactly opposite Demea at every point and so to force his brother into paroxysms of frustration. His reaction to Demea's outrage that Aeschinus's new wife and Ctesipho's slave mistress will share the same quarters is a good example:

DE: God Almighty, a courtesan and a matron in one house?

MI: Why not?

DE: Do you think you're sane?

MI: I believe so.

DE: God save me! When I see your idiocy, I think you're doing it to have somebody to sing with.

MI: Why not?

DE: And will the new bride learn this same stuff?

MI: Of course.

DE: You'll hold a rope and dance between them?

MI: Exactly!

DE: Exactly?

MI: And you with us if we need somebody.

DE: Oh! Aren't you ashamed of this? (746–54)

Micio then tries to calm Demea, but not until he has treated him unmercifully. Surely, Demea deserves some of this kidding, but Micio is also protecting himself against his own unsureness. He too has worried about Aeschinus (cf. 150–54). Furthermore, Micio is not completely fair with Demea in his dealings with Ctesipho. He has objected to Demea's interference with Aeschinus (cf. 129–32), yet we find from Syrus that he not only approved of the handling of Sannio, but he provided money for the whole business (367–71). These can be seen as indications of what we might have suspected in general, that despite the soundness of his theories, Micio is eager also to have the favor of the young men to an extent that undermines our positive view of him.

We have seen in the section on structure how the play's last sequence brings these features of Micio's character into full view. Micio has acknowledged his willingness to support Aeschinus financially. Now we see him in short order agree to demolish walls, free slaves, give up farms, and even marry Pamphila's mother, Sostrata. If we are to take all this as fact, and the movement of the play gives reason to do so, we must see a father who has far too little confidence in his ability to secure his son's good graces without resorting to flagrant indulgence.

Aeschinus's character must be considered in the light of what we have seen in Micio. Micio has told us what he wants for the young man. Aeschinus represents a generally successful product of this system. He has inherited his father's leadership ability, as made clear by his quick action in helping his brother with the slave dealer. He has been resourceful enough to support Pamphila for some months. Certainly, his heart is in the right place. He is frantic that he should be thought to have abandoned Pamphila and eager to be considered reputable (cf. his "blush" at line 643). Furthermore, he has a genuine devotion both to Micio and to his brother Ctesipho.

On the other hand, Aeschinus is rather wild, so much so that even Micio is worried. He is self-indulgent, apparently, to an extent that would suggest to cooler heads than Demea's that he has been spoiled. His treatment of Sannio should be viewed critically. The humor of the scene, and the unsavory reputation of the slave dealer's trade, cannot completely obscure the fact that Aeschinus has carried away Sannio's rightful property in a very high-handed, not to say illegal, fashion. The slave dealer is in a business without great dignity, in ancient or modern times, but he is a legitimate tradesman, and yet Aeschinus does not scruple to have him restrained forcibly. The slave dealer cannot really press charges because young men are good customers despite the aggravations of dealing with them, and so for the sake of business he routinely puts up with outrage.

In his father's own terms Aeschinus is not perfect. Micio highly prizes communication between father and son. On the important matter of Pamphila's pregnancy, however, Aeschinus is not frank with him. It is for this principally that Micio chides him in their confrontation. Finally, should we be in doubt about Aeschinus's being spoiled, the play's final segment shows us this side of his character in vivid detail.

Demea, Ctesipho, and Syrus. Demea is seen always in direct or implied comparison with his brother. Until the last he is consistently the same character, uniformly reacting extravagantly to each new twist of Aeschinus's story. That is not the trait, however, for which we would censure him. Rather, this tendency to rise to any bait is treated comically. Demea is, after all, the play's "blocking character," so that his broadly sketched character is functional within the overall plan for humor.

We must be more repelled, however, by his self-assuredness about his own rectitude and the success of his program with Ctesipho. He refers constantly to Ctesipho's virtues and the tightness of his own control over him:

If he [Aeschinus] needs an example, doesn't he see that his brother pays attention to business, lives in the country frugally and sober? (94–95)

Would I allow him [Ctesipho] (to do something disgraceful)? Wouldn't I have sniffed it out six months before he began anything? (396–97)

Such self-ignorance under the circumstances is culpable. The difference between the real Ctesipho and Demea's concept of him is our strongest evidence for the weakness of his theories of childraising.

Whereas Aeschinus is a generally successful young man, confident, decisive, and considerate, despite his self-indulgence, Ctesipho is timid and something of a sneak. His adolescent interests are similar to those of his brother, but he cannot manage his own affairs. Aeschinus may be unwilling to go to his father with everything as Micio would prefer; Ctesipho is afraid for Demea to know anything of his true nature.

A key to understanding the problem in the relationship between Ctesipho and Demea can be found in Syrus's role. If Demea assumes the position of obdurate father, Syrus plays the clever slave. Although he does not scheme for money, he is instrumental in helping the young men with their difficulties. In Ctesipho's case, however, his most prominent service is in keeping him out of trouble with his father. In the process he shows us many of Demea's faults, as when he parodies the old man's sententiousness (419 ff.). He does this most effectively by playing on the old man's own treasured misconceptions of Ctesipho. When Ctesipho is panic-stricken that his father will find him, Syrus assures him that Demea is easily handled:

SY: But just relax. I know the way he is quite well. When he's at fever pitch, I bring him down quiet as a lamb.
CT: How?
SY: He loves to hear you being praised. I make out to him that you're a regular god. I tell him your virtues.
CT: Mine?
SY: Yours. Like a little boy he sheds tears of joy down his face. (533–37)

Ctesipho then withdraws and allows Syrus to deal with his father for him.

Syrus's strategy is, in fact, to keep father and son apart as much as possible. He tries to send Demea off to the country and does succeed in leading him on a wild goose chase. He stands, often literally, between the two so that they never communicate directly. Demea is content to form his opinion of his son chiefly on reports of a go-between, who has been anything but frank with him. Communication becomes a principal issue, and in this area the results of Demea's efforts are clearly inferior to those of Micio.

Sannio and Hegio. Of the minor figures two, Sannio, the slave dealer, and Hegio, the relative of Sostrata, deserve some mention. Both are traditional types, but their contributions to the whole are indicative of the careful characterization in *The Brothers.*

As we have seen, Sannio is borrowed from a play by Diphilus. Through their interaction with him we get our first view of Aeschinus, Ctesipho, and Syrus. He establishes himself as a stock figure from his own lips: "Aeschinus, listen. Don't say that you didn't know how I am. I'm a slave dealer" (160–61). "Slave dealer" (*leno*) is title enough to tell the audience everything. He plays his role consistently, not apologizing for his trade but giving no reason for anyone to cheat him, and so underscoring Aeschinus's high-handed notion that he and Ctesipho should have exactly what they wish.

Hegio is also a stock figure, the poor but respectable citizen (cf. Demea's assessment, 438 ff.). The solidity of his character makes him a perfect foil in meetings with both Demea and Micio. His good character reflects on Sostrata's reputation and so helps to assure us that Pamphila is indeed a proper wife for Aeschinus, despite her poverty.

Theme.   Theories of childraising are on review in *The Brothers;* this much is obvious. What the play has to teach us about this subject, however, is a more controversial question. The evidence of the play itself has been interpreted in radically different ways, nor is there agreement on cultural and political considerations that might affect our view.

It is perhaps best to schematize baldly the most commonly held line of argument. Micio and Demea disagree on method; we have the results of their theories on display in Aeschinus and Ctesipho; Aeschinus is clearly better adjusted and happier with his father than is Ctesipho; therefore, the play favors Micio's approach generally, although the ending reminds us that no theory is good if pursued to the extreme and that we must temper Micio's view with Demea's.

Dissenters can be found going in opposite directions from the center. Some would deemphasize the notion of compromise, preferring to see the play's ending as reflecting more on Demea's clumsiness than on Micio's weakness. Others believe that the last section makes clear that Micio has spoiled Aeschinus completely through his permissiveness and in fact Demea represents the sounder route.

An appeal to the Terentian biography might be useful in establishing a context for the play's theme. If we accept as fact Terence's close association with the Scipios—and we must recall that the connection is by no means sure—then it is tempting to posit the struggle between the fathers in political terms. Micio represents a liberal attitude in opposition to staunch conservatism as shown by Demea. Now, Demea would fit well with stereotypes of the conservative Roman, as represented by the faction of Cato. The Scipionic faction, on the other hand, was committed to the changing Rome of the expansion period after the Second Punic War (201 B.C.). The "moderating" ending can also be accounted for in this way, for liberal politics does not wish to be considered as intent on destroying old values, but on improving upon them.

We should also consider in a more general cultural sense the possible impact of the play on its audience. By any standard, Catonian or Scipionic, second-century B.C. Rome was a conservative community. Certainly Demea's conservative outlook would not appear regressive, as it might to a modern audience educated on popular psychology with its concerns for child development. It is also possible that the Roman would be even more sensitive than a modern reader to the issue of money. Micio argues in part that he will support Aeschinus (and Ctesipho) because he can afford to do so. He argues that his and Demea's less wild youths were the result more of poverty than disinclination. Second-century B.C. Rome was very concerned with how to accommodate newly acquired prosperity without doing complete violence to cultural values forged in much more frugal times. Finally, one aspect of the play that is subsumed under the larger theme of childraising is that of communication between parent and child. A modern audience will surely be sensitive to this issue in a more systematic way than would an ancient one because of the emphasis in professional circles upon effective interpersonal communication. In any period, however, this is an interesting and important subtopic of the childraising issue.

In the final analysis, the issues of the play are clear, and we will form our opinions principally on the evidence presented in the drama itself. The play goes to great pains to show us the type of men who are espousing these opposing theories and the results of them, the "proof of the pudding," in the form of the two children. In fact, Micio himself says that both children will do fine, that neither is ruined (820 ff.), and so we might well expect that a compromise is the logical solution to an unhappy choice between extremes. Still, for all his spoiling, Aeschinus must be considered a better developed person than his brother. Ctesipho is capable of devotion to his brother and affection for his uncle, but he is clearly stunted by Demea's handling of him. In fact, we are hesitant to accept the conventional, and obvious, interpretation of the play chiefly because of the last segment, in which Demea's actions seem to wreak havoc with what has gone before. From our previous examinations of this section, however, we can say that it is not so unexpected as it might appear at first glance. Throughout the play Terence has shown us weaknesses in Micio and strengths in Demea. He has also been quick to bring in farcical elements. That Micio should have his comeuppance from Demea, who has been the chief sufferer up to now, and that this should be accomplished in a farcical manner is consistent rather than surprising. Thus, we can martial strong support for the view that the play espouses a compromise between the ideas of Micio and those of Demea, but one that lies much closer to Micio's view than his brother's.

Chapter Five

Terence and His Influence

Terence has left us six plays upon which to base our evaluation of him. If, as the tradition affirms, this is the total output of his short life, we are in a position to survey his work without the worrisome question of how we would modify our opinions if we had more complete evidence. His reputation as a comic dramatist has withstood the test of critical opinion through the centuries; his theatrical soundness is evidenced by the influence he has had on playwrights since the Middle Ages, who turned to him for the most practical of reasons, that he provided characters, themes, and comic formulae useful for reaching their own audiences.

We have examined in detail Terence's career and his individual plays. In this summary chapter we will look at his accomplishments in a more general way and examine his principal themes. In addition, we must give some indication, however briefly sketched, of his enormous influence on Western drama.

Terence the Dramatic Artist

Style and Characterization. Since antiquity Terence has been especially prized in two areas, the refinement of his style and the care with which he fashioned characters. It is difficult to demonstrate how one must conclude that style is excellent and characters are handled well without resorting to close analysis of specifics. We can, however, delineate Terence's chief strengths without going on at great length.

Style. Terence's Latin is a model for educated speech of the second century before our era. His language is idiomatic and appropriately chosen to fit mood and character. Nor is it only the opinion of modern scholastics. Roman critics were quick to cite his excellence in use of language. Whereas his older second-century B.C. colleague Plautus reveled in highly lyrical passages and extravagant verbal effects, Terence was controlled. Though less lyrical, he managed spoken meters skillfully and reproduced the idiom of the educated upper class in smooth dramatic poetry. Thus, not only has he been used as a model for school children in search of a good Latin style, but those playwrights well versed in Latin have found him a study in dialogue construction.

At another level, Terence managed the pace of his dialogues with great craft. It has long been a canon of good dramatic structure that material should not exist for its own sake, but should contribute to character or plot or theme, preferably to all at once. Both within the individual scene and in the ordering of scenes Terence's touch is deft. His plays are all quite short, none over 1,100 lines. Yet he managed to get the most out of each scene so that we are left with complete, well-turned plots and characters effectively developed. Such was his control of when, how, and with whom characters should speak.[1]

Characterization. Ever since the Roman scholar Varro credited Terence with Roman comedy's best characters, critics have given our poet high marks for his handling of character. The French critic Diderot might have been speaking for the critical tradition at large when he wrote, in his essay "Praise of Terence":

What man of letters has not read his Terence more than once and does not know him almost by heart? Who has not been struck by the truth of his characters and the elegance of his diction? Wherever in the world one carries his works, if there are libertine children and angry fathers, the children will recognize in the poet their follies and the fathers their reprimands.

Certainly, Terence emulated models which had carefully drawn characters, but he did not follow any model slavishly and his own skill in this area was considerable, so that his characters are always prominent in our consideration of a play.

Terence's genre, in fact, puts special constraints upon the playwright, for it relies totally on stock types for each play. No character in Terence is, then, wholly unique. There are old men, young men, slaves, matrons, courtesans; but no carpenters, insurance salesmen, maniacs, or the like. The skillful playwright, however, turns this to his advantage.

Since the basic outlines of a role are recognized immediately by an audience, the playwright can create most of his characters quickly so that he can concentrate on "individualizing" a specific example of a type, needing only spare space to accomplish much. Terence was masterful at this manipulation of his genre, and was able not only to fashion "interesting" stock characters but to make them function in the larger framework of his theme.

One technique he favored was the use of pairs from which comparisons might be made to reveal the nature of each role. Thus, for example, we develop our opinion of Micio and Demea, the two old men in *The Brothers,* from seeing them constantly in relation to one another. The same is true of Menedemus and Chremes in *The Self-Tormentor.* Terence also accentuates the strength of one important character by placing it against the weakness of a less significant, similar figure, as, for example, the young man Pamphilus in *The Girl from Andros,* who gains stature from comparison with his friend Charinus, or Aeschinus, the strong-willed young man in *The Brothers,* who is seen in relation to his brother Ctesipho.

Often minor figures are given just the touch of personality necessary to raise them from the level of dramatic ciphers to characters who enrich the overall texture of the play. Thus Bacchis, the courtesan, and Antiphila, the ingenue, in *The Self-Tormentor* have minor roles, and each is a stock type, but in their interaction they gain depth and help to place the actions of others in perspective. The serving girl Pythias, who might well have remained a nondescript slave, exhibits a strength of purpose that accentuates the theme of *The Eunuch* in such a way as to make it a significantly better play. Minor female characters such as Nausistrata, the deluded wife in *Phormio,* and Myrinna, one of the wives in *The Mother-in-Law,* are likewise used effectively to show the injustices in these plays; male characters such as Hegio in *The Brothers* and Crito in *The Girl from Andros* become effective instruments for giving credibility to information or individuals.

Because his plays lacked expository prologues and so needed to develop character and situation internally, Terence expended special effort on his opening scenes. In three of these he made use of protatic characters, introduced as foils for a principal figure and then allowed to drop from the play: Sosia, the freedman who talks with Simo at the beginning of *The Girl from Andros;* Geta, the slave who talks with Davus to open *Phormio;* Philotis, the young courtesan, and Syra, the old maid, who are prominent in the first scenes of *The Mother-in-Law.* These minor figures are developed just enough to provide from their interactions with major characters important thematic and character information, and the care with which they are employed is sound testimony to Terence's skills.

Themes. If Terence has been prized for his characters, he must nonetheless be singled out also among the playwrights, ancient and modern, of the New Comic tradition for the richness of his themes. Except for *Phormio,* his plays develop ideas worthy of serious comment and consideration. We have dealt with the individual plays elsewhere. At this point we may consider Terence's themes in a more general way.

Terence and "Theme" in New Comedy. To the extent that the plays of New Comedy deal with the foibles of everyday people, they may be thought to "hold the mirror up to nature." It is possible, then, to find in almost any play elements that can be seen as corrective satire or models for moral edification. The fact that bourgeois problems are lifelike, however, is not by itself sufficient reason to take the situations of these plays seriously.

Hence, there has been a tendency in modern times to judge New Comedy more on style than content. Aristophanes depicts specific social and political problems; New Comedy thrives on generalities. But to the ancients New Comedy was considered highly instructive; Menander above all others was thought to provide a view of existence from which we could profit, but no less a conservative Roman than Cicero was interested in Terence's plays for the examples he might find there. And, as the passage from Diderot quoted above would suggest, serious critics in other eras have found Terence worthy of their careful consideration.

In fact, Terence is at pains to elevate issues which in other circumstances might have remained at a level of trivial importance to a genuinely serious plane. This very tendency has often been adduced as a criticism of his comedy. He can wax subtle, so that his plays often have rather little of the obvious humor we associate with the comic stage. The advantages of less obvious humor and of profounder moods must be weighed against this loss of verve and a tendency to moralize. Not all critics have found that balance in Terence's favor.

Taken as a whole, however, theme remains in the opinion of most a strength of Terentian comedy. He does not write philosophical plays dedicated to expounding a systematic view of life, albeit philosophical ideas in common circulation in the Hellenistic world are found in his work. Rather, when he has completed his presentation, the characters have been rich enough, and the complications of their interactions sufficiently understood, so that we see a common problem in greater depth. The focus is not on theoretical social, political, or psychological issues, but the investigation of ordinary interpersonal situations.

Fathers and Sons. The single most common situation in New Comedy is that of a young man in love but unable to pursue his affair happily, primarily because of his father, who will not pay the expenses or disapproves of the relationship. It is not surprising, then, to find fathers and sons in all of Terence's plays. In his treatments, however, we are shown important rather than routine aspects of their relationships.

The Girl from Andros, The Self-Tormentor, and *The Brothers* all make the father-son relationship their central concern. Miscommunication is generally the cause of problems, arising both from faulty parenting and from the generation gap. In *The Girl from Andros* old Simo is so fearful that Pamphilus is ruining his life by devoting himself to Glycerium that he cannot grasp that his son's character is really quite solid. He is dominated by his fears and becomes obsessed with forcing his son into a relationship with a more acceptable girl so that he loses his sense of balance. Ironically, the son acts more responsibly than the father, and only the typical ending in which Glycerium is found to be an acceptable marriage partner after all can salvage the situation.

The Self-Tormentor presents a different sort of problem. One father, Menedemus, is so remorseful at having been too unyielding and thereby driving his son into the army that he racks himself daily with hard labor; his neighbor, Chremes, is the repository of all good advice and is eager to help Menedemus manage his relationship when his son suddenly returns. With typical comic irony, however, Chremes is in need of advice himself when he becomes aware that his own son is pursuing an affair with an extravagant courtesan. Again, lack of communication between well-meaning parents and their sons creates conditions dangerous to all their happiness.

The Brothers is the *locus classicus* for the father-son theme. Here, opposing extremes of childraising are at issue: Micio's permissiveness is pitted against his brother Demea's strictness. The play is so constructed that these relationships become tightly entwined. The children, Aeschinus and Ctesipho, are both the natural children of Demea. Aeschinus was adopted by Micio, however, and so there are two sets of brothers and two father-son relationships to provide many contrasts. Micio thinks Demea regressive, while Demea believes his brother is ruining Aeschinus. In the end neither father is totally vindicated. Ctesipho's independence has not prospered under Demea's handling. Instead, he has tried to hide his juvenile foibles and has made a mess. Aeschinus has fared better, but he too is not perfect. Furthermore, neither father communicates as well with his son as one would like. Ctesipho is afraid to reveal himself to Demea at all, and Aeschinus is not totally frank with Micio. Terence contrives to show us that both approaches must be tempered. He favors liberality generally, but warns against the dangers of assuming too much when dealing with adolescents.

In the final analysis, it is indicative of the strength with which Terence manages his themes that we do not find a heavily moralizing tone. Rather, he has taken comic commonplaces and focused our attention on them, especially through the interactions of well-drawn characters, in such a way that we ponder the situations with some seriousness despite the comic atmosphere and the stock nature of the plot.

Humanitas. We must conclude upon examining Terence's plays as a whole that the father-son relationships we have just reviewed are only one aspect of a larger concern with human relationships in general. Some commentators have felt, in fact, that Terence's interest is in the nature of a philosophical position, that men should practice *humanitas,* or "humaneness," toward one another.[2] There is no need, however, to claim any organized philosophical approach for Terence in order to affirm that he was especially interested in the way people treat one another and the ironies inherent therein.

Each of the plays (except *Phormio*) examines human interactions under difficult conditions. We have noted the father-son relationships in *The Girl from Andros, The Self-Tormentor,* and *The Brothers.* In *The Girl from Andros* we see further how concern and love for others are expressed by different people. Ironically, the son, Charinus, is more effective in his protective love for Glycerium than is his father in his efforts to protect his son, for Simo, constrained by his own opinions of correct behavior, cannot separate his own frustrations from his view of his son. So, Simo cannot see how capable his son really is. For comparison, incidentally, we see Simo's friend Chremes find a much more satisfactory balance between concern for his daughter and for his friend's problems.

The Eunuch presents a counterpoint to genuine love in a play which shows the effects of human selfishness. Its characters profess devotion, but upon any close scrutiny we see them follow their own interests. The centerpiece for this examination is the callous rape of Pamphila by young Chaerea, who then claims without remorse that he is deeply in love with her. This message is softened by boisterous scenes which keep us well within the comic world, but Terence orchestrates them in such a way that the ending leaves us aware of the irony in what the characters say.

In *The Self-Tormentor* Terence explores the irony of a man, like Chremes, who is so interested in the affairs of others that he cannot see his own problems. We are edified by watching the relationships between fathers and sons in the play, but standing beyond this theme is the spectacle of Chremes falling into one of life's more common traps.

Terence's most ambitious effort in examining human relationships is *The Mother-in-Law.* We have seen in our section on that play how problematic it has been for critics who have discussed its dramatic viability. And yet, the play contains some of Terence's most attractive characters and the richest mixture of human relations of all his works. *The Mother-in-Law* shows us people being unjust to one another because of a willingness to believe wrong information or to form faulty conclusions rather than to trust the goodness of those close to them. Thus, everyone is confused by the strangeness of the situation. Philumena must feign reasons for leaving her mother-in-law when she finds herself pregnant. Pamphilus cannot accept the psychological burden placed on him by his young wife's problems, though he loves her a great deal; furthermore, he is caught between wife and mother. The old men are all too eager to assume that their children's problems stem from a mother-in-law's interference. Terence evokes pity, concern, and indignation as the play progresses, and it is only careful blending of comic elements with these somber concerns that keeps us attuned to the comic mood. In the end the genuine love and concern which the characters also show toward one another triumph in what remains Terence's most mixed comedy, but a truly interesting play.

Terence's Influence

Terence's influence on Western comic drama has been immense. He survived through the ages whereas his Greek predecessors did not, or, in the case of Aristophanes, were not rediscovered until the influence of the Roman playwrights had established itself firmly. Plautus, his immediate predecessor on the Roman stage, may rival him in influence, but in those periods when tastes favored urbane, sophisticated comedy, Terence was considered the master both for practicing dramatists and theorists alike.

Our survey of Terence's influence must be quite brief. Certainly, many sources are available which deal with his influence at greater depth, both in general and specific terms.[3] Here we will discuss briefly only two features of his influence, his place as a theoretical model and the direct use made of his plays by some later writers.

Terence as a Model for Comic Play Writing. The history of Terence as a model for drama is long and rich. It begins in the tenth century with a nun in Saxony, one Hrotsvitha, who wrote several plays to elucidate Christian virtues for the good of Christian maidens; she used as her model the comedies of Terence. In the Renaissance the notion that plays based on his comedies could be effective as moral statements was revived, and Terence was so favored as a model that scholars speak of a "Christian Terence."

In the sixteenth century not only practicing playwrights, especially in Italy, but schoolmasters and critics as well turned to the Roman dramatists, especially Terence, for evidence to support their dramatic theories. The *editio princeps* of his plays published in 1470 made him generally available, and the ancient commentaries on his work survived, especially that of Donatus. Thus, Terence became a model against which to measure the theories of Aristotle and Horace, and the Terentian commentators also gained stature as theoreticians. As Marvin Herrick puts it,

the Athenian Aristophanes was too vulgar, too indelicate; the Roman Plautus was sometimes too vulgar and often too "irregular." The later Roman poet, Terence, offered safer and more familiar ground upon which schoolmasters and critics could expatiate on art, on manners, and on morals.[4]

Terence was a favorite source for the playwrights of the later English stage, who often waxed theoretical about their work. William Congreve (1670–1729), for example, specifically states that he was the inheritor of Terence's stage; he was typical of those writing comedy of manners in this era.

In the eighteenth century, the great Frenchman of letters, Denis Diderot (1713–1784) credited Terence as a near-perfect model for the aspiring comic playwright. He wrote several essays on drama in which he cited Terence frequently as illustrative of his notions of how comedy should function. Diderot's impact on practicing playwrights and critics throughout Europe was considerable. His fondness for Terence is best expressed in his short essay "Praise of Terence" (ca. 1769): "Young poets, alternately turn the pages of Molière and of Terence. Learn from the one to draw, from the other to paint." Diderot felt secure that Terence's lack of comic energy was more than compensated for by his refined diction and his great skill in character portrayal.

Terence and the Comic Playwrights.   It is an old saw that good playwrights borrow, great playwrights steal. Even a quick glance through literary history confirms that comic dramatists have always been alert to good material and willing to appropriate it regardless of its source. The list of works which have used Terence's plays directly is quite long, and the reputations of their authors great. We need cite only a few examples to give a clear idea of the extent of his influence.

Molière has two works based closely on plays of Terence. *The Brothers* was the principal model for *The School for Husbands* (1661); *Phormio* provided the core (around which was wound material from many other places) for *The Trickeries of Scapin* (1671). In fact, Plautus appealed to the great Frenchman more than did Terence, but the influence of Terence's dramatic style on his work was significant. For example, *The Miser* (1668) was based on Plautus's *The Pot of Gold,* again with material from several other sources. Now, *The Pot of Gold* has what Terence would have called a "simple" plot, that is, it has one love affair. Molière made his play "double," as Terence might have said, that is, he introduced neat pairs of characters in two intertwined love affairs. Terence made great use of such technique, and became a prime model for such composition for later playwrights. Thus, in *The Miser* Molière followed a tradition going back to Terence: he turned a single plot into a double one and in the process "Terenced" Plautus.

Terence's influence on Shakespeare is less direct. The Englishman, like Molière, seems to have gone to Plautus more. We can feel confident, however, that Terence had an effect on Shakespeare's dramatic thinking, for he must have read him quite as much as Plautus.

In England during the seventeenth and eighteenth centuries, when the stage was filled with comedy, Terence found many admirers. We have mentioned Congreve's "spiritual" affinity to him. More direct influence can be found in *The Squire of Alsatia* (1688), by Thomas Shadwell, or Richard Steele's *The Conscious Lovers* (1722), the first based on *The Brothers,* the second on *The Girl from Andros.* Other examples might be easily cited from an era in which the most popular comedies were akin in theme and character to the bourgeois atmosphere of Terence's plays.

In modern times Terence, as well as Roman comedy in general, has lost the position of direct influence on practicing playwrights, though Roman drama is still taught in history of drama courses. Occasional revivals have been successful, but they are novelties that are meant as adaptations. The heirs of Terence have had their influence, however, and comedy of manners is still very popular whether in the theater, at the movies, or on the television "sit-com." Terence remained a basic author in the schools until perhaps fifty years ago. No one at the opening of Oscar Wilde's *The Importance of Being Earnest* (1895) would have missed the humor arising from the careful reincarnation of Terence's brand of New Comedy. The bourgeois situation, the "duality" construction with its two interconnected love affairs, and the improbable recognition scene can be understood immediately as coming from Terence as much as from Wilde's predecessors on the British stage.

Notes and References

Abbreviations

Beare, *RS:*   W. Beare, *The Roman Stage: A Short History of Latin Drama in the Time of the Republic,* 3d ed. (London: Methuen, 1964).

Duckworth, *NRC:*   George E. Duckworth, *The Nature of Roman Comedy: A Study in Popular Entertainment* (Princeton: Princeton University Press, 1952).

Norwood, *AT:*   Gilbert Norwood, *The Art of Terence* (Oxford: Blackwell, 1923).

Chapter One

1. As examples one might cite the balanced account of Duckworth, *NRC,* p. 56 ff. See also the presentation by G. Jachmann in Pauly-Wissowa, *Realencyclopädie der classischen Altertumswissenschaft,* s.v. *P. Terentius Afer* (1934), col. 600, and the summary of the careful commentary on the *Life* by Nicola Terzaghi, *Prolegomeni a Terenzio* (Torino, 1931; Rome, 1970), pp. 39–40.

2. Terzaghi's discussion of the life (*Prolegomeni,* 26 ff.) considers the question of sources carefully. The great literary scholar Marcus Terentius Varro (116–27 B.C.) has been suggested as the source for the core of Suetonius's work. His involvement would lend an air of authority to the material; however, most scholars now feel that Suetonius was working with a later compilation. He quotes half a dozen or so of his sources by name.

3. For example, Duckworth, *NRC,* p. 57. The first edition of the *Oxford Classical Dictionary* (1949; Oxford: Clarendon Press, 1953) lists ?195–159 B.C., while the second edition (1970) opts for ca. 190–159 B.C. Sidney G. Ashmore in his introduction to *The Comedies of Terence* (New York, 1908), p. 26, prefers 185 B.C. as does J. Marouzeau, *Térence: Comédies* (Paris, 1942; reprinted 1947), p. 9.

4. The most extreme statement of this "agnostic" premise, one that was not pressed by its author in his later work, is W. Beare, "The Life of Terence," *Hermathena* 59 (1949):20–29. (See his reconstruction of Terence's life in *RS,* pp. 91–95).

5. See Gilbert Norwood's elegant appraisal of the aridity of the *Life* in *AT,* p. 132.

6. Such was the suggestion of Tenney Frank, "On Suetonius' Life of Terence," *American Journal of Philology* 54 (1933):272–73.

7. Norwood (*AT,* p. 132) refers to him as "possibly a mulatto or quadroon."

8. In the midst of an article that questions many basic assumptions about the chronology of Terence's plays ("The Terentian *Didascaliae," Atheneum,* n.s. 37 [1959]:148–73) Harold Mattingly remarks, "Our closest authorities identify these friends as Scipio and Laelius and we can surely accept them as correct" (p. 164). See *The Oxford Classical Dictionary,* 2d ed., under "Scipionic Circle."

9. The prologue of *The Brothers* tells us that Terence appropriated a scene from Diphilus. This bit of information is not preserved by the *didascaliae.*

10. Perhaps there was a revival in 146 B.C. (cf. Ashmore, *Terence,* p. 82).

11. For example, an important manuscript variation in the *didascaliae* of both *The Eunuch* and *Phormio* reverses their order. Donatus in commenting on *The Brothers* tells us it was acted second, though scholars argue that he meant this as played after the second attempt to produce *The Mother-in-Law* on the same program at the funeral games for Lucius Aemilius Paullus. On a small point, Donatus's record of the notice of *The Girl from Andros* (the *didascalia* itself has been lost) makes Flaccus the son of Claudius.

12. H. Marti provides a convenient overview of the scholarly debate in his bibliography "Terence 1909–1959," *Lustrum* 8 (1963):30–33.

13. See, for example, T. F. Carney, *P. Terenti Afri Hecyra* (Pretoria: Classical Association of Rhodesia and Nyasaland, 1963), p. 22.

14. Mattingly, *"Didascaliae,"* pp. 154–56.

Chapter Two

1. The text followed is that of Robert Kauer and Wallace M. Lindsay (Oxford: Oxford University Press, 1926). Translations are those of the author. The poetry of Terence's plays is rendered here as prose so that there is no attempt to duplicate the text by poetic lines.

2. For discussions of this possibility see Terzaghi, *Prolegomeni a Terenzio,* p. 35; G. Jachmann in Pauly-Wissowa, *Realencyclopädie der classichen Altertumswissenschaft,* col. 600, and Mattingly, *"Didascaliae,"* p. 160.

3. There has been no general agreement on what is meant by

contaminare (or the noun *contaminatio*, not found in the ancients but generally used in modern scholarship). See the summaries by Beare, *RS*, pp. 310–13, and his article "Contamination," *Classical Review*, n.s. 9 (1959):7–11.

4. We find no evidence that copyright gained legal status in Rome, but certainly the guild sought to protect its interests de facto. For Terence and the establishment see E. G. Sihler, "The Collegium Poetarum in Rome," *American Journal of Philology* 26 (1905):1–21. On the general concept of "copyright" see W. Beare, "Recent Work on the Roman Theater," *Classical Review* 51 (1937):106–7.

5. Terzaghi, *Prolegomeni*, pp. 34, 37. For the traditional view see Duckworth, *NRC*, p. 61.

6. See the modern appraisals and analyses by Norwood, *AT*, pp. 89–90, and Duckworth, *NRC*, p. 149.

7. The *didascalia* says that the first time it was acted "without a prologue." But cf. Carney, *P. Terenti Afri Hecyra*, p. 22: *"sine prologo:* there must have been a prologue to the *Hecyra* at its first production. . . ."

8. Cf. Beare, *RS*, p. 165.

9. A good presentation of the position that the failures of *The Mother-in-Law* should not be ascribed to dramatic flaws is Kenneth M. Abbott's oral paper "What Happened to Terence's *Hecyra,"* Classical Association of the Middle West and South, April 1980. Both Terzaghi, *Prolegomeni*, p. 54, and Mattingly, *"Didascaliae,"* pp. 166–67, support the view that Terence's bad luck was caused by his enemies.

10. Mattingly, *"Didascaliae,"* p. 163.

Chapter Three

1. Beare, *RS*, pp. 10–23, offers a convenient overview of this early Italian dramatic history. That these few pages can encapsulate the information pertinent to this material is an indication of the sparsity of our information.

2. Although the Athenian tradition is that best known to us, there was a thriving independent tradition in Sicily. Its best-known playwright was Epicharmus (fifth century B.C.). Very little is known of this form, though some have thought that a play from it was the source for Plautus's *Amphitruo.*

3. Lily Ross Taylor, "The Opportunities for Dramatic Performances in the Time of Plautus and Terence," *Transactions of the American Philological Association* 68 (1937):284–304, presents the most thorough account of the circumstances of dramatic performances in the Roman republic.

4. These four types certainly encompass the range of theater

popular in Rome. The question may be somewhat more complex, for the terminology used to refer to them was varied. See Beare, *RS,* Appendix D, pp. 264–66.

5. Beare, *RS,* p. 39.

6. A few lines of Plautus's *Bacchides* are based on a surviving fragment of Menander's *Twice Tricked* (*Dis Exapaton*). The most interesting example is that left us by Aulus Gellius in *The Attic Nights* (2.23) comparing Caecilius Statius and Menander with regard to *The Necklace.*

7. The classic treatment of this subject remains Eduard Fraenkel, *Elementi Plautini in Plauto,* trans. Franco Munari (Florence: La Nuova Italia, 1960; orginally *Plautinishes im Plautus* [Berlin: Weidmannsche Buchhandlung, 1922]). There is a thorough, balanced survey of the topic in the long essay by Konrad Gaiser, "Zur Eigenart der Römischen Komödie," in *Aufstieg und Niedergang der Römischen Welt* (Berlin: Walter de Gruyter, 1972), vol. 1, pt. 2, pp. 1027–1113.

8. A work that explores the evidence such as it is in an effort to give a coherent picture of the *palliata* playwrights and their individual accomplishments is John Wright, *Dancing in Chains: The Stylistic Unity of the Comoedia Palliata* (Rome, 1974), American Academy Papers and Monographs, vol. 25.

9. See the impressive list of Romans who talk of him in Beare, *RS,* pp. 86–90, and Wright, *Dancing,* p. 87.

10. The study that explores the relationship between Terence and the poet's guild is E. G. Sihler's "The Collegium Poetarum at Rome," *American Journal of Philology* 26 (1905):1–21. For recent additions to the arguments see N. Horsfall, "The Collegium Poetarum," *Bulletin of the Classical Institute of the University of London* 23 (1976):79–95.

11. Varro's remarks are quoted in Nonius, *De compendiosa doctrina,* p. 596 Lindsay; cf. Horace, *Epistles,* 2.1.59.

12. A convenient survey of the types can be found in Duckworth, *NRC,* p. 236 ff.

13. Wright, *Dancing,* e.g., pp. 58–62, maintains that the style that became standard with Plautus dominated later tradition.

14. Wright, *Dancing,* p. 87 ff., examines the question of Caecilius Statius's place in the tradition. His conclusions are somewhat at variance with the more generally received opinion.

15. Wright comes to the conclusion after a careful study of all the *palliata* fragments that Terence is much more innovative than his predecessors, who made their contributions rather closely within the framework as they found it. His full discussion of Terence is found in *Dancing,* p. 127 ff.

Chapter Four

1. Two well-known, and widely cited, works by T. B. L. Webster exhibit this tendency; while they are directly concerned with Greek playwrights, they spend a great deal of time examining plays by Plautus and Terence: *Studies in Menander,* 2d ed. (Manchester: Manchester University Press, 1960), and *Studies in Later Greek Comedy* (Manchester: Manchester University Press, 1953).

2. An alternative ending, comprising several lines meant for insertion near the end of the play, has survived in our manuscripts. These lines are post-Terentian, probably from the second century of our era. They are of interest on two grounds: that these lines survive suggests a continued history of production for the play, and they illustrate the extent to which the resolution of Charinus's suit for Philumena weighed on some later editor or director. The brief statement that the young men should seek Chremes inside to settle the matter was not enough, so a brief interchange with Chremes on stage was inserted. See Otto Skutsch, "Der zweite Schluss der *Andria,*" *Rheinisches Museum* 100 (1957):53–68.

3. There have been those who doubt Donatus on this point. Cf. Terry McGarrity, "Thematic Unity in Terence's *Andria,*" *Transactions of the American Philological Association* 108 (1978):111 and n. 22.

4. For a treatment of this method of composition see Duckworth, *NRC,* pp. 184–90. The important early statement of the concept and an analysis (not always generally accepted) of its importance for evaluating Terence is made by Norwood, *AT,* pp. 143–44 (for example). A useful effort to examine the effects of this structure even further is Richard Levine's "The Double Plots of Terence," *Classical Journal* 62 (1967):301–5. Levine does not discuss *The Girl from Andros* precisely because he sees this as a "first tentative approach" (p. 301, n. 2).

5. Most technical studies of Terence deal with this question. A useful summary is found in Duckworth, *NRC,* pp. 61–65.

6. See the discussion by McGarrity, "Thematic Unity," pp. 106–8.

7. There is evidence to suggest that as a convention things said about a character not on stage are usually closer to the truth than those said in his presence. The conversation is all the more useful, therefore. See Ortha L. Wilner, "The Technical Device of Direct Description of Character in Roman Comedy," *Classical Philology* 33 (1938):20–36.

8. One remembers that Varro ranked him first in characterization. Denis Diderot wrote of Terence: "What man of letters is there who has not read his Terence more than once, and who does not

know him almost by heart? Who has not been struck by the truth of his characters and the elegance of his diction? Wherever in the world one carries his works, if there are libertine children and angry fathers, the children will recognize in the poet their follies, and the fathers their reprimands" ("Praise of Terence").

9. Cf. Norwood's one-sentence verdict on the play: "It is plainly the work of a brilliant beginner: the Latin is charming, there are excellent speeches, the dialogue is clear and nimble; but the characterization is weak, the construction faulty" (*AT*, p. 23).

10. This observation, which plays an important part in the argument that follows, is derived from McGarrity, "Thematic Unity."

11. This is a point carefully discussed by McGarrity, "Thematic Unity," pp. 106–9.

12. Cf. Gordon Williams, *Tradition and Originality in Roman Poetry* (Oxford: Oxford University Press, 1957), pp. 401–2, where he wrongly describes Chrysis as Glycerium's mother.

13. Norwood, *AT*, pp. 23–24.

14. A brief description of the types is given by Duckworth, *NRC*, pp. 249–53.

15. Norwood, *AT*, p. 30, expresses the common prejudice: "In any play or novel it is poor art to base any important change upon some person or fact hitherto entirely unknown or unsuspected: it should be brought about by a character or fact familiar from the outset, but the import of which has not been realized."

16. We should remember that the Roman head of family was responsible, and derived his power, under a concept known as *paterfamilias*. This "father of the family" was a role that implied responsibility for a number of persons: e.g., wife, children, slaves.

17. Northrop Frye, *Anatomy of Criticism* (Princeton: Princeton University Press, 1957), p. 163 ff.

18. Cf. Beare, *RS*, p. 103: "The complications of the plot are difficult to follow on the stage, or even in the study; but there is evidence that the play was produced more than once, and we must applaud the public who could appreciate it."

19. The divergence of scholarly opinion on the question can be readily observed by comparing E. Lefèvre, "Der *Heautontimorumenos* des Terenz," in *Die römische Komödie: Plautus and Terence* (Darmstadt, 1973), pp. 443–62, and W. Steidle, "Menander bei Terenz II," *Rheinisches Museum* 117 (1974):247–76. Lefèvre favors the view that Terence made rather radical changes; Steidle argues for a more conservative view, that the modifications were not too profound.

20. Cf. above, note 4.

21. See the analysis of W. Beare, "*Choroû* in the *Heautontimorume-*

nos and the *Plutus,"* *Hermathena* 74 (1949):26–38, and H. W. Prescott, "Link Monologues in Roman Comedy," *Classical Philology* 34 (1939):1–23, 116–26, especially p. 120.

22. Such a view can be seen in the notation *Saltatio Convivarum* ("Dance of Banqueters") in the Oxford Classical Text after line 170, citing F. Skutsch, *"CHOROU* bei Terenz," *Hermes* 47 (1912):141–45.

23. Norwood provides a useful examination of strengths and weaknesses, *AT,* pp. 46–52, though, as usual, he relies primarily on taste as a canon.

24. Cf. Terzaghi, *Prologomeni a Terenzio,* p. 79: "Ma nemmeno Clitifone è cattivo: è vizioso e viziato. . . ."

25. See the discussion by Steidle, "Menander bei Terenz," pp. 247–49; but one might cite several other studies including H. D. Jocelyn, "Homo sum: humani nil a me alienum puto," *Antichthon* 7 (1973):14–46.

26. Cf. Steidle, "Menander bei Terenz," p. 275.

27. Cf. the evaluation of Duckworth, *RC,* 303–4.

28. An important early study of these problems is G. Jachmann, "Der *Eunuchus* des Terenz," *Nachrichten von der Gesellschaft der Wissenschaften zu Göttingen,* 1921, pp. 69–88. More recent are, for example, W. Ludwig, "Von Terenz zu Menander," *Philologus* 103 (1959):1–38; W. Steidle, "Menander bei Terenz," *Rheinisches Museum* 116 (1973):303–47; and H. Lloyd-Jones, "Terentian Technique in the *Adelphi* and the *Eunuch,"* *Classical Quarterly* 23 (1973):279–84.

29. Norwood, *AT,* p. 64 ff., finds many faults of construction, especially arising from the use of the characters of Gnatho and Thraso. E. K. Rand, "The Art of Terence's *Eunuchus,"* *Transactions of the American Philological Association* 63 (1932):54–72, represents an attempt to show the positive use of these characters. Kristine Gilmartin, "The Thraso-Gnatho Subplot in Terence's *Eunuchus,"* *Classical World* 65 (1972):141–45, also shows the complexity of their use.

30. The short essay of Douglass Parker as an introduction to his translation of *The Eunuch* (Palmer Bovie, ed., *The Complete Comedies of Terence* [New Brunswick, N.J., 1974], pp. 147–52) presents the core of a reading of the play, which shows the parasite's central place.

31. Cf. Norwood, *AT,* pp. 60–63. See another view in George M. Pepe, "The Last Scene of Terence's *Eunuchus,"* *Classical World* 65 (1972), pp. 141–45.

32. Charles F. Saylor, "The Theme of Planlessness in Terence's *Eunuchus,"* *Transactions of the American Philological Association* 105 (1975):297–311, makes use of this and other ideas of comic theory in his approach to the play (cf. pp. 306–7, 310).

33. Cf. Parker, *The Eunuch,* p. 150.

34. Cf. the works of Rand, Gilmartin, Pepe, and Saylor.

35. Those who have read Parker's introduction will note the influence of his ideas on the interpretation of theme presented here.

36. Norwood, *AT,* pp. 79–84.

37. There are a number of studies for which this is a central concern. A recent work bringing together and building upon this is Eckard Lefèvre, *Der* Phormio *des Terenz und der* Epidikazomenos *des Apollodor von Karystos,* Zetemata, 74 (Munich, 1978).

38. See Norwood, *AT,* p. 74: "In *Phormio* the momentous feature is that Terence's strictly dramatic power has come to maturity."

39. See Erich Segal and Carroll Moulton, *"Contortor Legum:* The Hero of the *Phormio," Rheinisches Museum* 121 (1978):277–78.

40. This point is effectively made by Segal and Moulton, "Contortor Legum," pp. 286–88, though their conclusion is marred by a ready acceptance of a "Scipionic" slant to the play, whereas the connection between Terence and the Scipios has never been conclusively established; see the discussion in chapter 1.

41. W. Geoffrey Arnott, "Phormio *Parasitus:* A Study in Dramatic Methods of Characterization," *Greece and Rome* 17 (1970):39. Quintilian was noted for his preference for Greek comedy over its Roman heirs.

42. Lefèvre, *Der* Phormio *des Terenz,* especially the section "Griechische Struktur und römische Struktur," pp. 92–96.

43. Segal and Moulton, *"Contortor Legum,"* p. 282.

44. See Arnott, "Phormio *Parasitus,"* pp. 32–33.

45. Cf. Segal and Moulton, *"Contortor Legum,"* pp. 285–87.

46. Cf. Lefèvre, *Der* Phormio *des Terenz,* p. 111.

47. See Lefèvre, *Der* Phormio *des Terenz,* pp. 102–8, for a discussion of this problem.

48. For a brief discussion of the problem see Carney, *P. Terenti Afri Hecyra,* pp. 146–47.

49. See David Sewart, "Exposition in the *Hekyra* of Apollodorus," *Hermes* 102 (1974):247–60, especially his concluding paragraph.

50. See W. Schadewaldt, "Bemerkungen zur Hecyra des Terenz," *Hermes* 66 (1931):1–29, especially the summary paragraph, p. 29.

51. See Sewart, "Exposition," pp. 257–58.

52. "In the whole comedy the action is managed in such a way that there is novelty, but not a complete removal from custom."

53. The two "failures" in Terence's lifetime have been much discussed. Donatus implies, in his brief addendum to Suetonius's *Life of Terence,* that the play was rarely acted later. Cf. also Norwood, *AT,* pp. 91–94, and Duckworth, *NRC,* p. 149. Norwood himself

was quite well disposed toward the play, accounting its failures an example of the unsophistication of Roman audiences.

54. Norwood, *AT,* p. 91.

55. Donatus calls her a "good courtesan" (*meretrix bona*). What he may have meant by this is not sure, but certainly she is not of the grasping sort seen in many of Plautus's plays. For a full discussion of her role see D. Gilula, "The Concept of the *Bona Meretrix.* A Study of Terence's Courtesans," *Rivista di Filologia e di Istruzione Classica* 108 (1980):42–65.

56. The scholarship on *The Brothers* is sufficiently varied so that rather than attempt to identify the source of various "strands" of interpretation, which may be espoused in several studies, it seems best to present an overview in this one place. Of great help in following the line of opinion on the play are two bibliographical studies: H. Marti, "Terenz 1909–1959," *Lustrum* 8 (1963):72–79, and Sander M. Goldberg, "Scholarship on Terence and the Fragments of Roman Comedy: 1959–1980," *Classical World* 75 (1981):96–100. These sources give, of course, a complete bibliography for the play; they also provide brief surveys of the items listed.

Of the many studies devoted to this play, several merit special mention, especially in light of the discussion presented here. Norwood's essay, *AT,* pp. 106–30, remains useful, and it is a good representative of those who warmly affirm the play's artistry. Two full-length studies have been influential: O. Reith, *Die Kunst Menanders in den* Adelphen *des Terenz.* Afterword by Konrad Gaiser (Hildesheim, 1964), and V. Pöschl, *Das Problem der* Adelphen *des Terenz,* Sitzungsberichte der Heidelberger Akademie der Wissenschaften, Philosophhistorische Klasse, 4. Abhandlung (Heidelberg, 1975). Pöschl is an example of those who support Micio's position in the play. Support for Demea can be found, for example, in W. R. Johnson, "Micio and the Perils of Perfection," *California Studies in Classical Antiquity* 1 (1968):171–86. For a study that deemphasizes the importance of the play's ending, see N. A. Greenberg, "Success and Failure in the *Adelphoe,*" *Classical World* 73 (1979–80):221–36. Finally, a study that attempts to place the play in a historical context is P. MacKendrick, "Demetrius of Phalerum, Cato, and the *Adelphoe,*" *Rivista di Philologia e di Istruzione Classica* 82 (1954):18–35.

Chapter Five

1. Gilbert Norwood is especially adept at discussions of style and dramatic construction. His *The Art of Terence* contains many analyses of specific examples illustrating well Terence's skills.

2. Cf., for example, Norwood, *AT,* p. 150 ff., or Duckworth's

remarks, *NRC,* pp. 303–4. H. Marti devotes a section of his bibliography to this topic, "Terenz 1909–1959," *Lustrum* 8 (1963):91–93.

3. A convenient compendium of the influence of Plautus and Terence can be found in Duckworth, *NRC,* pp. 398–441. His bibliography on this topic is also useful (pp. 462–64). Those interested in Terence's impact on the Renaissance will find instructive M. T. Herrick, *Comic Theory in the Sixteenth Century,* Illinois Studies in Language and Literature 34, 1–2 (Urbana: University of Illinois Press, 1950).

4. Herrick, *Comic Theory,* p. 5.

Selected Bibliography

PRIMARY SOURCES

1. Editions and commentaries

Ashmore, Sidney G., ed. *P. Terenti Afri Comoediae. The Comedies of Terence.* 2d ed. New York: Oxford University Press, 1908.

Carney, T. F., ed. *P. Terenti Afri Hecyra.* Proceedings of the African Classical Association, supp. 2. Pretoria: V + R Printers, 1963.

Donatus, Aelius, and Eugraphius. *Commentum Terenti.* Edited by P. Wessner. 3 vols. Leipzig: Teubner, 1902–1908.

Kauer, Robert; Lindsay, Wallace M.; and Skutsch, Otto; eds. *P. Terenti Afri Comoediae.* Oxford Classical Text, rev. ed. Oxford: Clarendon Press, 1958.

Marouzeau, J., ed. and trans. *Térence: Comédies.* Association Guilliame Budé. 3 vols. Paris: Les Belles Lettres, 1942–49; reprinted with addenda and corrigenda, vol. 1 (1947), vol. 2 (1956).

Martin, R. H., ed. *P. Terenti Afri Adelphoe.* London: Cambridge University Press, 1976.

———. *P. Terenti Afri Phormio.* London: Methuen, 1959.

Sargeaunt, J., ed. and trans. *Terence.* Loeb Classical Library. 2 vols. Cambridge: Harvard University Press, 1912.

Shipp, George, ed. *P. Terenti Afri Andria.* Melbourne: Oxford University Press, 1960.

2. Translations

Bovie, Palmer, ed. and trans.; Carrier, Constance, trans.; and Parker, Douglass, trans. *The Complete Comedies of Terence.* New Brunswick: Rutgers University Press, 1974. Verse translations.

Copley, Frank O., and Hadas, Moses, trans. *Roman Drama.* Library of Liberal Arts. Indianapolis: Bobbs-Merrill, 1965. Prose translations by Copley.

Radice, Betty, trans. *Terence. The Comedies.* New York: Penguin, 1976. Prose translations, useful introduction.

SECONDARY SOURCES

1. Bibliographies
Goldberg, Sander M. "Scholarship on Terence and the Fragments of Roman Comedy: 1959–1980." *Classical World* 75 (1981):77–115. Annotated bibliography with excellent critical summaries of the state of scholarship on many topics in Terentian studies.
Marti, Heinrich. "Terenz 1909–59." *Lustrum* 6 (1961):114–238. Bibliography of specialized topics such as textual criticism.
————. "Terenz 1909–1959." *Lustrum* 8 (1963):5–101; (addenda) 244–64. Continuation of the preceding bibliography, devoted to more general topics; useful annotated surveys of the state of scholarly opinion on many facets of Terentian studies.

2. Books and periodical Articles
Beare, W. *The Roman Stage: A Short History of Latin Drama in the Time of the Republic.* 3d ed. London: Methuen, 1964. Conservative, sensible survey of Roman drama; most authorative single source for stage practices.
Büchner, Karl. *Das Theater des Terenz.* Heidelberg: Winter, 1974. Somewhat ponderous, but recent and authoritative; examines all the plays closely and is an excellent compendium of opinion on technical questions.
Duckworth, George E. *The Nature of Roman Comedy: A Study in Popular Entertainment.* Princeton: Princeton University Press, 1952. The single most valuable source for Roman comedy; balanced surveys of all important issues in the study of Terence and Plautus.
Greenberg, N. A. "Success and Failure in the *Adelphoe.*" *Classical World* 73 (1979–80):221–36. An interesting approach to the problems created by the ending of *The Brothers.*
Jachmann, G. "P. Terentius Afer." In *Realencyclopädie der classischen Altertumswissenschaft.* Edited by A. F. Pauly and G. Wissowa, A. Reihe, vol. 5, pt. 1, coll. 598–650. Stuttgart: Metzlersche, 1934. Often cited and influential as a standard view of technical questions.
Konstan, David. *Roman Comedy.* Ithaca: Cornell University Press, 1983. Although focusing more on Plautus than Terence, has interesting essays on *Phormio* and *The Mother-in-Law.*
Lefèvre, E. "Der *Heautontimorumenos* des Terenz." In *Die römische Komödie: Plautus und Terenz.* Darmstadt: Wissenschaftliche Buchgesellschaft, 1973. A study of Terence's techniques of adaptation, with many sensitive observations on his dramatic construction.
————. *Der* Phormio *des Terenz und der* Epidikazomenos *des Apollodor*

von Karystos. Zetemata, 74. Munich: Beck, 1978. Very like the author's study of the *Heautontimorumenos.*

McGarrity, Terry. "Thematic Unity in Terence's *Andria.*" *Transactions of the American Philological Association* 108 (1978):103–14. An interesting attempt to evaluate the play's theme.

Mattingly, H. "The Terentian *Didascaliae.*" *Athenaeum,* n.s. 37 (1959):148–73. A closely argued critique of the traditional chronology of Terence's plays; presents a convincing hypothetical dating quite different from that of the tradition.

Norwood, Gilbert. *The Art of Terence.* Oxford: Blackwell, 1923. Opinionated and dated, but sensitive, especially on matters of style and dramatic technique.

Parker, Douglass, trans. Introduction to *The Eunuch.* In *The Complete Comedies of Terence.* Edited by P. Bovie. New Brunswick: Rutgers University Press, 1974. Though a short essay, very helpful in defining the play's theme.

Pöschl, V. *Das Problem der* Adelphen *des Terenz.* Sitzungsberichte der Heidelberger Akademie der Wissenschaften, Philosoph-historische Klasse, 4. Abhandlung. Heidelberg: Winter, 1975. An important study of the play's characters concentrating on Terence's modifications of Menander.

Reith, O. *Die Kunst Menanders in den* Adelphen *des Terenz.* Afterword by K. Gaiser. Hildesheim: Olms, 1964. Similar in method to the study just cited, but arriving at different conclusions.

Schadewaldt, W. "Bemerkungen zur *Hecyra* des Terenz." *Hermes* 66 (1931):1–29. A summary of the principal structural problems which have dominated discussions of the play.

Segal, Erich, and Moulton, Carroll. "*Contortor Legum:* The Hero of the *Phormio.*" *Rheinisches Museum* 121 (1978):276–88. An attempt to establish a theme for the play in its approach to the law.

Steidle, W. "Menander bei Terenz." *Rheinisches Museum* 116 (1973):303–47.

———. "Menander bei Terenz II." *Rheinisches Museum* 117 (1974):247–76. Both close analyses of Terence's dramatic techniques, with good interpretative comments.

Terzaghi, Nicola. *Prolegomeni a Terenzio.* 1931. Reprint. Rome: Bretschneider, 1970. Important for its critical appraisals of many problems associated with Terentian studies; has had considerable influence.

Wright, John. *Dancing in Chains: The Stylistic Unity of the "Comoedia Palliata."* Papers and Monographs of the American Academy at Rome, 25. Rome: American Academy, 1974. A careful appraisal of Terence's place within his dramatic tradition.

Index